Praise for *Unstoppable Mindset*

"Alden Mills gives you the tools to develop the mindset you need to climb all of life's mountains (no matter how steep), and this book will help you every step of the way!"

—Allison Levine, *New York Times* Bestselling Author, *On The Edge*, and Team Captain, American Women's Everest Expedition

"*Unstoppable Mindset* is a guide on how to make your dreams a reality and your life an extraordinary adventure. I have known Alden since I hired him from Carnegie Mellon graduate business school in 1991 and watched how he has applied his Navy SEAL training to his own life and coached others to success.

Now is your chance to learn from one of the best leaders and motivators in the world if you are serious about success. He teaches you how to converse with yourself, maintain a positive attitude, and enjoy the work, the struggles, the victories, and the defeats necessary to create the life you want."

—Bart O'Brien, Cofounder, RSA Data Security and Calico Commerce

"Alden Mills is one of my favorite mental toughness and peak performance thinkers. In *Unstoppable Mindset*, he tells us that we are more powerful than we realize, then gives us a practical, step-by-step guide to activate our Heroic potential. I highly recommend this book for everyone looking to forge the mindset we need to make a difference in the world."

—Brian Johnson, Founder and CEO, Heroic Public Benefit Corporation, and Bestselling Author, *Areté: Activate Your Heroic Potential*

"In *Unstoppable Mindset*, Alden challenges you to truly Dream Big and then take comprehensive actions to fulfill those ambitions. Embracing the mind-body connections to deliberately build your positive mindset loop, control your focus and beliefs, and channel your energy into persistence will give you the courage to pursue your goals.

Alden shares his journey through the daunting challenges of Navy SEAL training and entrepreneurship, and reveals his essential components of a comprehensive system for a successful mindset. Deliberately building an Unstoppable Mindset with attention to sleep, exercise, breath, beliefs, discipline, and focus, Alden shows you that your dreams are worth pursuing and that with deliberate goal setting you can overcome any obstacle to reach your personal summit."

—Eric Hall, Chief Marketing Officer, Digital Experience Business, Adobe Inc.

"I have had the privilege of learning so much from Alden—in moments of joy, in moments of service, and in some of my most difficult times. He helps you become a better leader and in his latest book, *Unstoppable Mindset*, he shares all his tools to unlock the leader inside of you. This is more than a mindset book; it is a leadership manual to activate your potential. He inspires you to take your innate superpowers (we all have them) and be unstoppable!"

—Jennifer Crisp, Chief Talent Officer, Paul Hastings LLP

"Through inspirational personal storytelling of overcoming obstacles, former Navy SEAL and successful businessman Alden Mills provides a tactical, step-by-step guide for 'mindsetting,' revealing the profound power of our brains over our physiology. The fascinating connection between our thoughts, emotions, and attitude is the key to unlocking our personal potential and long-term dreams. For anyone eager to live an 'epic life, make your heart sing' or answer the question of what you would do if you knew you would succeed, this book is a must-read."

—Margi Power, Cofounder and Copresident,
Leadership Council San Mateo County

"Scaling a business requires a can-do, play to win, never-give-up mindset where you look at obstacles as opportunities and see the possibilities in problems. There is no better book to help you and your team develop an Unstoppable Mindset than the one in your hands. I have seen Alden in action—his mindset techniques are proven and effective, even with teenagers! Read this book, embrace his tools, and you will not only be ready to scale your business but also your life!"

—Verne Harnish, Founder, Entrepreneurs' Organization, and
Author, *Scaling Up* and *Mastering the Rockefeller Habits*

"Packed with engaging stories, this is a must-read for anyone looking to dream bigger for their life and career. Alden is our personal 'swim buddy,' pushing us to work hard and strengthen the most important muscle: our mindset."

—Mark Lipscomb, VP Global Talent and
Employee Experience, Adobe Inc.

"I have served in the Navy for 33 years and commanded a Carrier Strike force of more than 7,500 people, and I can tell you *Unstoppable Mindset* is a mission critical book to help you lead yourself and others to mission success. Whether you serve on the front lines for your country, corporation, community, or family, this book will help you find success. It worked for me and it can work for you!"

—RADM C.J. Sweeney, NIMITZ Strike Group Commander, U.S. Navy

"I tend to be an anxious, fear-based person. I've often thought that I'm just wired that way and won't change. Through my work with Alden and this book, I've come to see that much of that is a choice, and with a different approach and the techniques he recommends I can transform my mindset. Alden has helped me reframe how I see myself and move from being reactive to proactive."

—The Rev. Chris Rankin-Williams, Rector, St. John's Episcopal Church

"Alden Mills continues to help me be a better leader and father by identifying the important building blocks of life, and then simplifying them. More than a book, *Unstoppable Mindset* offers a manual for leadership both at work and at home."

—Rich Peterson, Cofounder, Lighthouse Public Affairs LLC

"Alden can help you architect your dream life. He is a master of empowerment and helping people think big. Over the course of one year, he transformed our private equity partnership using the approach laid out in this book. With his guidance, we unlocked our individual superpowers to achieve a collective strength unknown to us before. The work we did with Alden enabled our dreams. We often lose imagination as life progresses. This book can refresh the mindset and provides a framework to achieve goals initially thought too great and ambitious. Captain your ship, chart the course of your dreams, and let Alden guide you."

—Samarth Chandra, General Partner, Enhanced Healthcare Partners

"Simply put, Alden Mills is a world-class teacher, and his principles are dynamite—especially for teams bent on innovation. My team has used the techniques from this book to improve our mindset, persist, and innovate. When the going gets tough, we now say, 'Unstoppable Mindset!'"

—Shane Snow, *Forbes* Journalist, Bestselling Author, and Cofounder, Contently

"Alden's book is a passionate testimonial to understanding the *mindset* necessary to become *unstoppable*. Each page is dedicated to inspiring oneself to take action through purposeful exercises and tools to enlighten your mind. The stories shared educate the reader on how to establish meaningful goals that embody the compassion, respect, love, and balance needed to live your dreams."

—Stephen Revetria, President, San Francisco Giants

"My long-time swim buddy Alden has let you in on his secret to success with this book! I have known Alden since we were teens at the Naval Academy, graduated SEAL Training together, deployed together as SEALs, and have continued to be friends and business colleagues since our service. My favorite thing about Alden is his ability to tell a story that is both captivating and sincere. Everything he teaches in this book, I have seen him implement in his life for decades. Unstoppable Mindset training is a method of thinking and doing what works—*if* you follow his step-by-step instructions. Go get it done: PLAN, TRAIN, EXECUTE."

—Stew Smith, CSCS, Navy SEAL, Bestselling Author, and Founder, Heroes of Tomorrow

"Navy SEAL and successful entrepreneur Alden Mills is a living example that personal growth and achievement are earned with preparation, sacrifice, and unwavering perseverance. *Unstoppable Mindset* is brilliantly written and a must read! Alden Mills provides a pragmatic framework and useful tools to broaden our mindset to take action to achieve our goals and push beyond our preconceived limitations."

—Thomas J. Baltimore Jr, Chairman and CEO, Park Hotels and Resorts

UNSTOPPABLE MINDSET

Also by Alden Mills

Be Unstoppable
Unstoppable Teams

UNSTOPPABLE MINDSET

How to Use What You Have to Get What You Want

ALDEN MILLS

Matt Holt Books
An Imprint of BenBella Books, Inc.
Dallas, TX

This book is designed to provide accurate and authoritative information about personal and professional development. Neither the author nor the publisher is engaged in rendering legal, accounting, or other professional services by publishing this book. If any such assistance is required, the services of qualified professionals should be sought. The author and publisher will not be responsible for any liability, loss, or risk incurred as a result of the use and application of any information contained in this book.

Matt Holt is an imprint of BenBella Books, Inc.
10440 N. Central Expressway
Suite 800
Dallas, TX 75231
benbellabooks.com
Send feedback to feedback@benbellabooks.com

BenBella and *Matt Holt* are federally registered trademarks.

Printed in the United States of America
10 9 8 7 6 5 4 3 2 1

Library of Congress Control Number: 2023040630
ISBN 9781637744840 (hardcover)
ISBN 9781637744857 (electronic)

Editing by Katie Dickman
Copyediting by Ginny Glass
Proofreading by Becky Maines and Michael Fedison
Text design and composition by PerfecType, Nashville, TN
Cover design by Brigid Pearson
Cover image © Shutterstock / donatas1205
Printed by Lake Book Manufacturing

To those who believed in me when I did not, and to our four boys—H-master, Chow, Bear, and Yummy—who we believe in always.

We Love You,
Mom and Dad

CONTENTS

FOREWORD

I met Alden Mills in the fall of 1983. Alden was a freshman at Kent School in Kent, Connecticut, and I was a senior. Kent School is nestled into the bottom of the idyllic Housatonic Valley, with the Housatonic River flowing right next to the east side of campus. At the time, Kent had a reputation for being strict, and unlike in almost all other boarding schools, every student was expected to perform a daily job to support the campus community, whether it was clearing tables, cleaning dishes, sweeping hallways, shoveling snow, raking leaves, or anything else you could imagine to keep the campus pristine. I vividly remember meeting Alden in the dining room, where he was working on the cleanup crew, which was one of the *least* desirable jobs on campus. Just like the street sweeper in the Jimmy Buffet song "It's My Job," Alden had a hop in his step and was whistling away as he performed his job. The image of Alden's happiness while working such a dirty job always stuck with me, in part because of the contrast between what he was *doing* and how he was *behaving*. To this day, the image of him working in the dining hall at Kent makes me smile.

Although I am three years older than Alden, I followed his education and career from afar. I was not the least bit surprised to hear that Alden became an elite rower at Kent (a school known for its rowing), matriculated to and graduated from the United States Naval Academy, became a Navy SEAL team commander—an unusual career path for an Annapolis graduate—and then became the founder of the fastest-growing fitness-equipment company in the world. While his positivity and enthusiasm always suggested he would have a bright future, I had no clue what was really making him tick.

Fast-forward thirty-five years to 2018, and I find myself sitting across the table from Alden at a breakfast nook in Tiburon, California, where we both live. I had contacted Alden because one of his postings on teamwork caught my eye, and it helped me better understand the interpersonal dynamics of the team I was leading at my law firm. I was in a bad place and needed some advice. Alden shared the story of how he nearly dropped out of SEAL team training because of an asthma attack he'd suffered during a nighttime ocean swim, which he survived and completed thanks to the support of his "swim buddy." He then explained that the attrition rate of SEAL team candidates drops dramatically from the very moment they are paired with "swim buddies." At the end of breakfast, he offered to be my "swim buddy," and I accepted.

For the past six years, I have had the privilege of serving as the CEO of the North America region of Baker McKenzie, the leading global law firm, working closely with Alden for five of those years. I love my job, but it can be downright hard given the breadth of our law practices and operations, our matrixed structure, and a democratic culture where leadership can be called to account by the partners at any time. Over the last five years, Alden and I have discussed almost everything you are about to read in this book. To say these conversations have helped me lead and perform at optimal levels would be a massive understatement. For me, reading this book is akin to reading a chronicle of what I have learned from Alden.

Unstoppable Mindset is a must-read for anyone who is struggling personally or professionally—or both—as well as anyone who is thriving but wants to become even better. The content is too robust and rich for me to summarize here, but I will offer the following glimpse: One of the greatest challenges and impediments to success for many of us, myself included, is the ability to control our thoughts. Have you ever found yourself heading down a negative rabbit hole and said, "Don't go there," only to find yourself going even deeper and deeper? Alden argues that a combination of our thoughts, focus, and beliefs determines our direction in life and our careers, and he provides practical advice on how to quiet, if not get rid of, the "whiner" voice that resides inside of us. He explains that no matter who you are and no matter how successful, every one of us will encounter a moment of darkness in our lives, which can either be a golden opportunity or a major stumbling block *depending on our mindset.* In this moment, you—and only you—will make the difficult decision of whether you can or cannot take the next step forward toward achieving your goals and dreams. Alden will equip you with the mental and physical tools you need to take that critically important next step.

There is one other thing you should know about this book. We live in a society where our relationships with one another are becoming increasingly transactional, especially with the incessant distraction of social media and the interruption of electronic communication. It's hard to find much time to think, much less dream. Also, "dreaming" seems frowned upon these days, as dreamers tend to be considered less than serious people. (As Neil Young sings in his album *Harvest Moon*, "I'm a dreaming man, I guess that's my problem.") Alden challenges all of this because *he wants you to dream.* He wants you to envision your ideal life in one, three, or ten years from now and beyond, and he will help you attain your goals and dreams through daily practice and actions. He compares achieving your dreams to sailing across the ocean, knowing you can at best see three miles to the horizon and not know the turbulence that lies ahead. Of course, the first step to crossing the ocean is leaving the harbor, which means *starting* down the path toward achieving our goals.

In my own case, I left the harbor—a harbor of doubt—in 2018 at a coffee shop in Tiburon, listening to Alden regale me with the details of how his SEAL team swim buddy kept him from being dropped from the team straight to the rejection zone. I have since learned from Alden that pursuing my dreams is not very complicated, but it is definitely hard work. If you are ready to think, visualize, dream, launch from the harbor, and do the hard work necessary to achieve your goals and dreams, then you're in the right place with this book in your hands. I am confident it will help you as much as it helped me.

Colin H. Murray
CEO, North America
Baker McKenzie

INTRODUCTION

You Are More Powerful Than You Realize

I can remember the doctor's words clearly. "Mrs. Mills, your son has two problems," the pulmonologist said in a thick Boston accent as he picked up a couple of charts to show Mom my "problems." He looked like an older version of Danny DeVito with wispy white hair on the sides of his head, a shiny bald scalp on top, and thick convex glasses that made his eyes appear larger than they actually were. His resting facial expression looked as if he were smelling sour milk.

"Problem number one," he said while raising his index finger, "is he was born with smaller-than-average-size lungs." He held up a chart and pointed to a black dot well below a slanted black line that represented a normal twelve-year-old-boy's lung capacity. "And problem number two, he has asthma."

Then he said, "Here's what I recommend: he'll need to take medicine for the rest of his life, but he will also need to lead a less-active lifestyle. I suggest he learn how to play chess."

Upon hearing this initial diagnosis, Mom turned to me and said gently, "Alden, you go wait in the lobby. I'll talk to the good doctor alone now."

By the time Mom returned to the lobby, I had cried two small pools of tears onto the brown linoleum waiting room floor. She put her hands on her hips, nudged one of my feet with one of hers, and said, "What's wrong with you?"

I exclaimed with tears running down my cheeks, "Mom! Chess? I am terrible at checkers—how am I going to play chess!" My mind had already accepted the doctor's diagnosis, and I was already trying to cope with my new suggested reality.

Mom went into action. She had these long French-styled fingernails, and she filed them into fine sharp points to be used as literal attention grabbers for moments such as these. She dropped to a knee, dug one of her hands into my left forearm, and said, "Look at me, Alden."

I winced as I felt all five nails claw into my skin. "I'll get you the medicine, but you have a choice to make—the choice is deciding what you can or cannot do. No one decides what you can do *but you*—do you hear me?"

I grimaced and nodded, but I was more focused on her talon-like nails than her words, and she could tell.

She raised her voice and said, "Say it back to me!"

I was sure her nails were going to pierce my skin as I repeated her last sentence quickly: "No one decides what I can do but me."

"*Owww!*"

Of course, I did not understand what she was trying to teach me at that moment. I would have said anything to get her to release her grip. I did not get it that week or month, but over time, I did. She and Dad were very consistent on this message that "it's up to me to decide what I can do." Shortly after that doctor's appointment, I played for the YBA basketball team (I grew up going to our local

YMCA), my first athletic team, and the one basket I scored was for the opposing team.

Mom's response was simple: "So what if you scored for the other team? You scored. If at the end of the season you don't like basketball, then try another sport." She was relentlessly persistent and positive, reminding me that my only limitations were the ones I chose to set for myself.

She forever impacted my direction in life. Over more than forty years since that doctor's visit, I have struggled to pursue all kinds of dreams from athletic to military, business to community, and creative to family ones. I have at times failed spectacularly in the pursuit of my dreams, yet I learned how to press on, how to use those failures as fuel to become the captain of a nationally ranked Division I rowing team; get selected as a Navy SEAL platoon commander to lead three different SEAL platoons (earning a number one ranking as a platoon commander); build the fastest-growing consumer products company in the United States (number four on the *Inc.* 500); be awarded over forty worldwide patents; and—my greatest work-in-progress accomplishment—marry the love of my life and raise four boys who are courageously pursuing their own dreams.

I am acutely aware that I am the product of remarkable teachers who entered my life at just the right moments, from my parents to Olympic and national team rowing coaches; petty officers to master chiefs; warrant officers to war heroes, generals, and admirals; inspiring entrepreneurs and wildly creative artists; senior statesmen; movie directors; and orators. These relationships and many more supplied me with tools to help me convert obstacles into opportunities, see the possibilities in problems, and appreciate the advantages of adversity. These people were and are the masters of their crafts, and I feel so fortunate to have learned from them. This book is only possible because of them and their selfless coaching.

Though I may have distilled their teachings into these pages, please appreciate that we are all products of those from whom we are willing to learn. I was not always that willing, but their belief in me along with their patience prevailed. This book is my attempt to honor them while also acting as your swim buddy. In SEAL Team, no one accomplishes anything alone. We always have a teammate—called a swim buddy—who is by our side for the good times and, most importantly, for the great struggles. Every single success I have achieved was with a swim buddy. As you read this book, know that I am your swim buddy. I am here for you for each step and struggle you face.

Pursuing a goal—something you haven't done before and aren't sure you can do—is lonely business. It can be terrifying, and fill you with doubt. In fact, the single most important first step in the pursuit of your goal is "getting your mind right," as my SEAL commanding officers would say. But "getting your mind right" is not a destination; the process requires "getting your mind right" every day, every hour, and sometimes every second to press on—to keep giving it your all.

We are the products of our environments. We create our own limitations, and yet we are so much more powerful than we give ourselves credit for. Therein lies the irony of our situation. We have the ability to dream up amazing things in our lives, yet the same imagination we use to create our most desired futures can work against us to prevent us from realizing our true potential. To push beyond our boundaries while seeking that transformational goal, we need steady hands on our shoulders from trusted teammates who confidently and calmly remind us that we can do it.

Yet there are other moments of our journey into our unknown sea of capabilities when we need a drill instructor with a bullhorn driving us to push beyond our preconceived limitations. That is what I wish *Unstoppable Mindset* to be for you: your Navy SEAL swim buddy, who is *always* here for you, encouraging you to give more than you originally thought you could, and reminding you again and again that you can. It's no easy task to push yourself when your mind is screaming, pleading, and cajoling you to back off—to take the easy path—and to accept the average and find satisfaction with mediocrity.

Your success is dependent on your ability to adopt the mindset I have outlined in this book. *Unstoppable Mindset* will help you "get your mind right" and keep it that way throughout your journey to find the success you seek. I call this process of "getting your mind right" *mindsetting*. We all have the mindsetting capability and capacity to succeed; we just need practice.

I have designed this book to follow the Navy SEAL principles of mission planning. There are three basic phases of mission planning: plan, train, and execute. The chapters in this book follow the same format.

Chapters one and two represent the planning phase of your "mission"—achieving something you want (i.e., your goal). Just like in a SEAL mission, you must prepare your mind before you can execute the mission, and to do this requires proper planning. I will task you during the plan phase of this book to set your "mission"—to define the goal you seek to achieve.

Chapters three through eight introduce you to new mindsetting tools for training for your mission. There are exercises at the end of each chapter for you to use in your training phase—practice mindsetting by using these tools!

Chapter nine is where you'll put your training to work and begin going after something you want. You will have another opportunity to review your mission, and then it will be your time to execute.

You will never achieve an Unstoppable Mindset by sitting around and thinking about what you might be able to do—mindsetting requires you to take action, face the fear of failure, endure the embarrassment of trying new things, deal with the many demons of doubt, and grapple with your perceived limitations. These and several others are the many faces of fear, and they will be your greatest teachers as you deploy the tools in this book to build your own Unstoppable Mindset.

Will you fail? You bet! But when you finish this book you will come to realize that failure is only failing if you haven't learned anything from the experience of trying. Will you succeed? That's on you. I can tell you this: *you have all you need to succeed.* An Unstoppable Mindset is available to anyone who is willing to take the risk of trying to cultivate one.

I want you to dream audaciously and pursue your goals courageously. This book represents more than a tool kit. It is your swim buddy—this resource will always be here for you as you stumble and fail, doubt yourself, and question your abilities. I will remind you again and again that I believe in you and that you can do it—all you need to do is keep taking action.

LEAVING THE HARBOR

My clients span from individual CEOs, general managers, and EVPs running multibillion-dollar corporations and business units to entrepreneurs, private equity managing partners, and military leaders, and from small executive teams to massive audiences. The tools and metaphors I use can work for anyone. The metaphor I use throughout this book is a sea captain willingly leaving a safe harbor to reach a new destination far beyond the horizon. It's a powerful and relevant metaphor, for we are all "captains" of our own "ships" (our lives).

Ships are meant to be at sea. If they sit too long, the hull will attract barnacles and algae, which create more drag on the vessel and require even more energy to get it underway. Yet leaving a safe harbor can be a terrifying event. The unknown, which exists outside the safety of a harbor, presents all kinds of challenges—from unseen, submerged obstacles to the wind, waves, and sea currents. Much like life, all kinds of challenges arise when you decide to pursue something new.

Then comes the moment you lose sight of land while pursuing your course to your new destination. Loneliness, fear of the unknown, doubt, and many other challenges will confront you, working to convince you to turn back toward your harbor of familiarity. Much of this book is designed to help you overcome those many faces of fear so you will press on courageously in pursuit of your goal.

The task of "getting underway"—taking the initial action—is hard. Energy is required to go from a standstill to forward progress. In pursuing a dream, the energy used is mostly mental (even if your dream is a physical one, like training for a triathlon). Starting is inherently difficult because you are expending energy while not seeing any results. Your progress is limited, or there is no progress at all. (Try writing the first paragraph of your first book—I stumbled on this obstacle for a month!) I do not know the percentage of people out there who say they want to do something yet never take a single action to start, but it has to be high. (My informal marketing research of people telling me they wanted to be a SEAL or invent a product or write a book but never tried is over 50 percent.)

Starting the pursuit of your "new course" is hard because it requires you to believe in something you do not yet see. The old adage of "seeing is believing" is incorrect. You must first believe before you can actually see it. Believing is not easy. You must believe for quite some time before you can see the results of your efforts. Doubts are with us all the time, and they are one of the first mental obstacles we must learn to overcome in our journeys to success.

In the following chapters, every instrument, tool, framework, and technique I share is to help you dominate these doubt demons long enough for you to take action toward your goal. That's right: I said "long enough" because they never go away completely; the doubt demons are always with us. They are like our early-warning indicators of trouble ahead, and I will teach you how to harness them as fuel to keep persisting. Unfortunately, many people start their journeys only to be convinced by their doubt demons that their dreams are "not possible" or "silly," or that "they aren't good enough" or "it's not meant to be," or any number of other excuses. Taking action is the best defense against doubt. The challenge is that "doubt" will work overtime to convince you not to take that first action. But one action often leads to another, which eventually leads to progress—doubt's worst nightmare—and progress is where doubt-crushing confidence lives.

I love the ship metaphor, because we are all in charge of captaining our lives. This is our single greatest leadership responsibility: taking action in our lives. We are just like a real ship's captain: we must plan our courses, practice learning how to navigate our ships, and embrace the open water's challenges both foreseen and unforeseen. But most importantly, we must leave the harbor of familiarity, for the longer our vessel sits, the harder it will be to get underway again.

To help you get underway, I will help you get your compass heading set through proper goal setting. Once underway and outside the safety of the harbor, facing the elements of the ocean—wind, waves, and water (currents)—you will apply the same techniques and tools that I used to make it through SEAL training and to excel as a SEAL platoon commander and a CEO. You will learn how to overcome negativity by building your own Positivity Gym that will enable you to use failure, hardship, and obstacles as fuel.

I will help you create your Mindset Map so you can chart your path to success regardless of the sea state you face. When the currents seem too strong and you find your focus drifting to failure, I will teach you how to shift your focus back to getting on your course. You will gain frameworks and mindsetting tools to use our three critical mindset controllables—thoughts, focus, and beliefs—to Be Unstoppable at going after what we want. Most importantly, my focus is to inspire you to take bold action in the direction of your dreams. We are built for action, just as ships are made to be at sea. We know, when we are at sea, far from the safety of a comfortable harbor, we will learn the most about ourselves and create the greatest memories. At "sea" is where life is lived.

▸•◂

I harbor no ill will for the "good doctor," as my mother would refer to him, for he was trying to protect me by keeping me safe and out of harm's way. Yet here is the irony: "safe" is not what we are meant to be. We are built for the struggle. Struggle makes us stronger—it helps us move forward. I think of struggle like friction; without friction, we cannot advance. As one of my leadership coaches, John D. Messinger (Naval Academy '81), would remind me often: "If a car's wheels are on ice, the wheels spin, and the car doesn't move; wheels, like humans, need friction to move forward." Friction (or struggle) provides the traction to give us forward progress as an individual, team, organization, community, and even a country.

Yet, facing friction is hard. It's not normal for someone to willingly choose to embrace the struggle. It is especially hard to move from a place of comfort to discomfort. Why leave a perfectly comfortable lifestyle or place of safety to encounter the pain of perseverance (i.e., working hard, learning, failing, doubting, trying again, and perhaps even dealing with ridicule and embarrassment)? We are hardwired to avoid pain and pursue pleasure. However, the greatest and most rewarding pleasures follow the hardship of struggling to overcome adversity.

Why do some people willingly embrace the pain of forward progress while most sit on the sidelines accepting mediocrity and offering excuses for why they cannot succeed?

The short answer is mindset.

The people who make the choice to embrace the discomfort associated with success have flipped a switch in their minds correlating the pain of the current struggle with the payoff of future pleasure. Their mindset morphs obstacles into opportunities and problems into possibilities. They associate adversity with advantages, and struggles with building strength. Pressure becomes a privilege, and challenges are no longer avoided—they are welcomed and even sought out. I call these associations and others like them the definition of an Unstoppable Mindset. You build a habit of learning how to filter out the excuses of why you "can't" do something and constructively allow yourself to focus on the reasons why you *can*.

To our knowledge, we only have this one life to live, and we have no idea when it will end. So why not take full advantage of the time we have? And how do we do that? We use what we are born with and maximize our gifts for our full benefit to live epic lives. Which leads me to dreams. What does an epic life mean to you? What makes your heart sing? What would you do if you knew you would succeed? The very essence of the answers to each of these questions lives in your imagination, where your dreams are born. The point of this book and the reason for building your own Unstoppable Mindset is to live your dreams.

An Unstoppable Mindset is not reserved for those few who were born with some special persistence gene—it doesn't exist. An Unstoppable Mindset arises from making a choice to practice, to fail, and to push yourself beyond what you originally thought was possible, and then doing it again and again. As you learn to embrace the friction and feel the exhilaration of forward progress, you will come to realize that your potential is limitless. I strongly believe—and I have experienced this numerous times with both myself and others—that our human potential is so much greater than we realize. The challenge is activating our potential so we can experience it. Once you activate your potential (think of it like a snowball—the farther you push it, the bigger it becomes), your greatest challenge will be your imagination. You will discover the only limiting factor of your life is your imagination.

Adopting an Unstoppable Mindset means living a life where everything that you face is an opportunity to gain more pleasure—pleasure from learning, from getting stronger, from conquering obstacles, from doing things that have not been done before, from serving and helping others. To live that life, you must embrace a few simple mindset beliefs: we are imperfect, obstacles are opportunities, and we always have the final say in what we decide to do.

An Unstoppable Mindset enables you to tap into the power of your mind to make the choices that move you closer to the success you seek. *Unstoppable Mindset* is not just a step-by-step guide to help you chart your own course to success, but also a repository of inspiration with which to face and overcome fear along the way. Use this book as your guide to help you chart your course for new, bold destinations.

You are taking action by reading this book, and you are planning a course to change your life in all kinds of positive ways by coming to the realization that you are more capable than you know and you have untold power you have yet to apply. Navy SEAL Teams are made up of the smallest teams, each called a swim pair—two people—two swim buddies. I am now your swim buddy. I am here to help you activate your potential. I cannot wait to watch you soar. The world needs you at your best. Let's link arms, enter the water, and go build an Unstoppable Mindset!

Charlie Mike.

Alden

P.S. *Charlie Mike* is SEAL speak for Continue Mission.

1

What Is an Unstoppable Mindset?

"Sir, you gotta be kiddin', right?" said the lead machine gunner of SEAL Team Two's hotel platoon.

"Web, I'm serious as an ambush—take some time and really think about it before you answer."

Petty Officer Web (Web, for short) was not only the lead "60 gunner" (named after the type of machine gun, M60, he was expert at using), he was also my swim buddy. He remains an imposing man, standing over six feet three inches tall. All muscle, he could run and swim for hours and never seemed to be out of breath. He was one of the more reserved men in my platoon. He preferred to let his machine gun do his talking, and he knew how to "make his '60' sing," as he liked to say. But on this particular day, he did not have the cover fire of his weapon to help him with a goals exercise I was asking all sixteen men in my platoon to complete.

Hotel platoon was referred to as the "Hotel Hoggs" because physically we were one of the largest platoons in the compound. Several of my platoon mates, including myself, were "Clydesdales"—a SEAL who is over six feet in height and two-hundred-plus pounds. I earned the nickname "Boss Hogg," both for being the platoon commander and tipping the scales at over 255 pounds, making me the heaviest "Hogg" in the platoon. In the mid-1990s, a typical SEAL platoon schedule involved twelve months of training (called a "workup") followed by a six-month overseas deployment. We were in the first month of our workup when I handed out a single sheet of paper that was preprinted with the date, each platoon member's name, and three bullet points: five years, three years, and one year. You would hav I had just asked my teammates to go back through Hell Wee intense five and a half days of basic training during which you get a total of three and a half hours of sleep) when I asked them to take the weekend to fill out two personal and two professional goals for each of the three time periods.

I had spent the first five years of my SEAL career underwater as a mission commander for classified combat mini-submersibles called SDVs (SEAL Delivery Vehicles) at a command literally located next door to SEAL Team Two. I had led two platoons of SDVs. Hotel Hoggs was my first special-operations platoon. Most of the platoon had done at least one deployment together, and several had done multiple overseas tours. Everyone knew each other, except me—I was the outsider. And it certainly did not help their comfort level with me when I presented them with "goal" homework.

Since Web was my swim buddy, he had become more accustomed than most of the platoon to talking with me, hence his immediate, incredulous response to my request for his goals. Soon other platoon mates chimed in with statements like, "Boss, I don't do goals," or "Only goal I need is a mission, sir."

After a few more comments like these, I explained, "I hear you. I know this isn't standard operating procedure for you, but let me tell you why I want you to fill out this goal sheet. Goals do two things: one, they set your direction, helping you keep your focus, and two, they help me understand how I can help you."

Before any of them could offer more resistance, I said, "I want you to take the weekend to really think about where you want to be, what you want do five years from now, then I want you to answer the same for three years from now, and then one year. I want two personal and two professional goals for each time period."

h fifteen-minute time slots for the follow-
Web. "You don't have to share your goals
you do have to sign up for a fifteen-minute
h me next week."

as I said, "Oh, by the way, that's an order."

up for my first goal meeting on Monday morn-
ing. atoon hut so the meetings would be as private as possible. Web s ed as he handed me his goal sheet, saying, "Here ya go, sir—hot off the goal press."

He had written "Go Heavy, Go Hard, or Go Home" again and again and again.

"I like your mantra, but that's not a goal," I stated flatly.

I explained further. "Goals are something we can track. They come from something we imagine and desire in the future. I appreciate 'going heavy and going hard' (60 gunner slang for carrying a full complement of ammunition and then using all of it before returning to base), but I hate to break it to you that you will not be a 60 gunner for the rest of your life."

I pressed him, asking him what he really wanted in the future. I forced him to share something that he was passionate about. At first, it was a material thing—he wanted a customized truck he could sleep in on hunting and fishing trips while on liberty in his home state of Minnesota. After sharing the truck dream, other dreams seemed to flow a bit more. He wanted to try out for SEAL Team Six, earn the rank of master chief, and retire after twenty years of SEAL service.

He struggled to complete the goal sheet, like many before and after him, because he had not spent time really thinking about what he wanted in life. I get this tendency, especially when you are serving in the military, where one's mindset can become very focused on the next order or mission to complete. It can be very hard to consciously carve out time to think about what you want to achieve both personally and professionally. It's a selfish act to think about your goals. And selfish acts in SEAL Team are not high on anyone's priority list; after all, SEAL Team is about how you can serve the team, not about how the team can serve you.

There were a few other teammates who responded with similar mission-focused mantras, but then there were a few I will never forget, such as Petty Officer KD. He came to me somewhat timidly, which was unusual for him because he had been a Division I swimmer at Auburn University, and he was confident in most everything he did in and out of the water, including being the lead radioman of the platoon, a critical and highly technical role. Before he handed me his goal sheet, he fidgeted in his chair and leaned forward as if to whisper a secret to me, asking, "Sir, this meeting is confidential, right? I mean, you're not going to share these goals with anyone, right? Like, no one in platoon or even in the team, right?"

Using his nickname, I said, "KD, I promise this is between you and me only. I treat your goals as TS/SCI." (That's code for one of the highest levels of military classification: Top Secret/Special Compartmental Information.) He nodded and rubbed his hands on his thighs before asking me, "Sir, do you think I have what it takes to be an officer?"

My eyes widened. I leaned toward him and looked him square in the eyes. "KD, I absolutely believe you have what it takes, and I am certain you can do it if that is what you want."

I will never forget those goal conversations, especially the ones where they dared to dream audaciously. The bigger their dreams, the more I wanted to be a part of helping them succeed. Hotel Hoggs would be my last platoon. I made it my mission to help each and every one of my teammates with their goals before I left SEAL Team to head to business school and chase my own goals.

Can you guess what happened with Web and KD? If you guessed that Web would join the ranks of SEAL Team Six, become a decorated master chief, and retire after twenty-plus years, you guessed correctly. Two years later, I got a short note from KD: "I did it, sir—got picked up for the seaman-to-admiral program. Thanks for all your help." We lost touch as most SEALs do when you leave the teams. I do my best to track my "boys" from afar, and it wasn't too hard to follow KD, especially when he earned the rank of commander and became the commanding officer of a SEAL Team. The power of goals.

WHY GOALS MATTER

The purpose of this book is to help you achieve something you aren't sure you can accomplish. It's meant to help you manifest that figment of your imagination called a dream into trackable goals that eventually become your new reality. This chapter identifies and discusses the four steps of converting a dream into a goal. Goals matter because the process of defining and executing on your goals gives you focus, accountability, and clarity.

There are five important reasons goals matter, and I have made an acronym to help you remember their importance. I call the acronym GOALS, and here is what it stands for:

G—Give direction: goals give direction. Without goals, you are like a ship without a compass aimlessly sailing about and highly susceptible to the winds, water (currents), and waves. Our lives are filled with all kinds of distractions; we need all the help we can get when it comes to making a decision on where we spend our time and energy. That's what goals do; they give us direction like the North Star does for a navigator.

O—Offer accountability: the process of setting a goal spurs us to create accountability for pursuing it. The more we commit to the act of setting and communicating our goal, the more we build a commitment to work toward it. Share your goal with others, and your personal pressure to stick with the goal further builds a bond of accountability. Of course, the goal is yours, and so is your own accountability, but the more you commit to your goal, the more you will feel accountable to achieve it. (Tip: To improve your accountability, team up with a goal buddy—a swim buddy who keeps you accountable for taking action.)

A—Achieve more: people who set goals achieve more because they are more focused with their time. Goals help you manage your time, which enables you to maximize your efforts. One of the most overlooked and invaluable resources we have is time. Goals lead you to achieve more with the time you have.

L—Learn more: when you set a goal, you are setting yourself up for continually learning from how to achieve the goal more efficiently and learning how to overcome the obstacles that come with a goal. Goal setting naturally involves creating "friction"—the friction of learning/experiencing new things. The more goals you set, the more you learn what to do and, importantly, what not to do.

S—Serve as motivation: goals act as motivation. The fuel behind a goal is the ability to track your progress. The ability to see you are making progress toward your goal can act as powerful motivation to keep pressing forward. Even the slightest progress can be all the motivation you need to persist.

These are five of the more powerful reasons why I believe goals matter. You may have a glorious dream and a great vision, but neither matters unless you take daily action toward your dream, and that starts with setting daily and weekly goals.

OUR BRAIN ON GOALS

Having clear goals helps you channel your energy, attract the energy of others, and keep you inspired to persevere on your journey to achieving them. The bigger the goal, the more energy, support, and inspiration you will need, and the more important our mindsets become. Our brains are the most complex systems on the planet, so complex, in fact, that we still know very little about how they work. However, what we know today is leaps and bounds more than we knew as little as ten years ago. I am not a neuroscientist, but I will share a few neurological breakthroughs to help you understand (and believe) the immense power of what is housed between our ears and how to harness it to help you succeed.

We have essentially two main states of consciousness: conscious and subconscious.[1] The conscious state is what it sounds like: you are awake and going about your daily activities, such as eating, driving, working, playing, and so on. The subconscious state is operating most when we are sleeping, but we now know it is also operating while we are awake.

---

[1] Scientists will debate there are even more states of consciousness, but for our general working purposes, these are the main two.

Here's why it's important to know that your subconscious is always at work.

Our conscious mind can only handle a few tasks at any given moment. There is some debate as to how many tasks we can handle at once, but it's in the single digits.[2] That said, we still can only do one thing at a time really well. The moment we think we can do multiple things well is the moment we start performing suboptimally. While we go about our day working on all the tasks we decide are important to us, we have our subconscious operating systems working behind our consciousness. (Our brain is often compared to a computer. Where do you think the genesis of computer design came from? It was based on the operating system of what we know about our brain.)

Our subconscious is working on things that we have intentionally or unintentionally told it to work on. For example, have you ever told someone "not" to do something, only to watch them do it? The simple act would be something like this: "Henry [my son], don't spill your bowl of cereal as you bring it to the table." Within seconds, his overfilled bowl of milk and Cheerios rocks back and forth to cause a spill on the way to the breakfast table. Henry was not purposefully trying to spill his Cheerios, and I did not want him to spill them either, but what his "operating system" heard was "spill." Somewhere between the communication of his conscious and subconscious, the command "spill" became the focus.

Now let's take something a little more complicated, such as trying not to fail a class. In my first semester at the Naval Academy, I had it in my head that I was not good at math and so calculus was too complex for me to grasp. I kept telling myself all semester long, "Alden,

---

[2] Women score higher than men in their ability to multitask.

just don't fail calc." For weeks and weeks, the script I kept repeating was "don't fail." I can remember the phone call I received from the Naval Academy Academic Review Board like it was yesterday: "Midshipmen Mills, you are to report early from Christmas leave to attend an Academic Review Board."

"Oh," I said, then stuttered before feebly asking, "Ah, sir, how come?"

The senior officer responded flatly. "Anyone who fails a class must attend an academic review, and you failed calculus."

Another way to think about your subconscious activities and how they impact your outcomes is to imagine driving a car, or snow skiing in a heavily treed area. When you drive a car on a winding highway and steer through a turn, where should you be looking—into the turn or on the outside of the turn (where the guardrail or trees are)? Same goes for skiing in the trees—is it more helpful to look at the trees or the snow between them? The answers are obviously "into the turn" and the "snow between the trees." However, when we first learn to drive or ski in the trees, we must be much more intentional with our thoughts and actions. We need to learn a new set of commands that must be practiced before it becomes embedded into our subconscious. The first time you drive through a corner or ski through the trees requires a lot more conscious focus. The more we practice and reinforce the proper sequence of actions, the quicker the subconscious will get trained in new "commands." Over time, you will find yourself developing new habits that become automatic actions that occur at a faster pace than when our conscious mind methodically tackles a problem. The same rules apply when deciding to go after a new goal. At first, things are slow, methodical, perhaps even mechanical. You will find yourself needing to remind yourself why you are doing what you are doing to keep yourself on course.

Imagine you're trying to accomplish something that could take years to achieve such as "become a Navy SEAL platoon commander" or "make the *Inc.* 500 list" or "write a best-selling book" (all three of these were dreams of mine). If you do not have a system for "programming" your subconscious, you can find yourself in a constant tug-of-war between your subconscious and conscious actions. I think of the connection between our subconscious and conscious like being the captain of a ship. Your consciousness is making the decision about what course to take while your subconscious represents all the systems of your ship that will help you take that course. Systems such as your engine, rudder, throttle, steering, and compass are part of your ship's systems, which you need to help you stay on course. When they are in alignment with the captain (you), navigating your ship through high winds, rough seas, or strong currents is possible. But when they aren't in alignment, your ship can have a mind of its own. Imagine turning left, but your ship goes right. How frustrating would that be for you? How long would you try to keep pursuing your "course" (your goal) before returning to the calm, safe waters of home port (i.e., what you are familiar with)?

In other words, how long would you keep trying to pursue something if nothing seemed to be going your way? My point is you are in the captain's seat, but you need to know how to keep your ship on course in all sorts of conditions, and that takes practice.

Let me be clear. I am not implying that all you need to do is tell yourself, "I can do it," every moment of the day, and—*voilà!*—your proverbial ship is ready to take you to your desired destination (success). But I am saying we can learn to steer our ships with some specific techniques that will help optimize our chances for success. Getting our ship ready to set sail starts with not just setting goals but *how* we set those goals.

THE FOUR STAGES OF GOALS

There are four stages of goals: the dream, envisioning the dream, turning that vision into a goal, and taking daily action toward achieving the goal.

Stage One: The Dream

All goals start as a figment of our imagination. I call this "figment" a dream, a snippet of an imagined future state. Typically, dreams capture the end state of whatever our dream is, such as winning the game, achieving the award, earning the promotion, driving the sports car, or owning a certain house. Our ability to imagine is one of the critical differentiators that makes us uniquely human. This ability appears rare in animals outside captive situations and is primarily observed in great apes, parrots, and cetaceans.[3]

We dream up all kinds of things, and we are especially great at dreaming when we are children. Think back for a moment to when you were a kid. What did you dream about? Can you remember any of those crazy dreams you had, such as going to the moon or being a stuntman or fireman or perhaps a rock star and an astronaut at the same time? How about having a jet pack that you could use from your flying car after taking it for a deep dive in the ocean! Maybe your dreams were about creating masterpieces of art or rocking the world stage with your make-believe band or becoming a princess or the president of the United States.

---

[3] Robert W. Mitchell, "Can Animals Imagine?," in *The Routledge Handbook of Philosophy of Imagination*, ed. Amy Kind (London: Routledge/Taylor & Francis Group, 2016), 326–38.

Children dream with reckless abandon because they dream without constraints. To them, everything is a possibility because they have yet to accept a reality of limitations that adults have decided to accept. At some point on our paths to adulthood, those fantastical figments of our imagination get grounded in the reality around us. We shelve our dreams for more "realistic" expectations of what we might be able to accomplish. Those realistic ideals typically come from others before us who have either tried and failed to achieve a dream, or have determined through some type of scientific, mathematical, or logical process that said "dream" is not achievable.

I bring up this childhood to adulthood transformation to tell you it is a trap—a subconscious steering toward groupthink mediocrity. Just because you are an adult doesn't mean that you can no longer dream. In fact, part of the reason I am writing this book is to help inspire you to start dreaming with a vigor similar to that with which you used to dream as a child. It's still inside of you—it's just been locked away for a while.

Spoiler alert: I will ask you to conduct a goal-setting exercise at the end of this chapter and then again at the end of chapter nine. What you will find is your first set of goals will be more conservative than the second set of goals. Perhaps your goal is to learn Spanish and be able to speak it fluently. You set a goal to study Spanish thirty minutes a day using a language-learning app. By the end of this book, your goal might be to live in Spain with your family while learning and practicing your Spanish. You may have business goals, such as inventing a product and selling it around the world, or perhaps you want to write your own book or sail around the world or do both at the same time. Your goals are yours to imagine, and I am here to encourage you to dream without constraints and with reckless abandon.

Stage Two: Dream to Vision

A large majority of dreams never see the light of reality. Most dreams are nothing more than momentary delusions on which we have no intention of spending any more time than the moment we spent imagining it. Other dreams, however, become recurring thoughts that, with each passing remembrance, become more vivid and compelling. This transition stage is what I call "envisioning," a concept echoed in Nate Zinsser's *The Confident Mind*,[4] or turning a dream into a vision. Think of a dream like a highlight clip of a movie, such as the victorious outcome, the joyous triumph, or a happy ending. If the dream represents the highlight clip, then the vision is the highlight movie reel of your dream in Technicolor. The vision brings your dream to imaginary life. This is an important step of the alignment process between your conscious and subconscious, and it is also where I need to take some creative license with the ship metaphor.

In our make-believe subconscious ship, imagine that each component of our ship has a say in where our ship goes. They may not be able to completely change the direction, but they can certainly slow things down or cause breakdowns if the components are not all in alignment with the direction the captain (you) wants to go. Essentially, your ship and its components need to be told (and reminded repeatedly) where you want to go. This directional briefing between the conscious and subconscious is what "envisioning" does—it gets all the components of your ship in alignment with your destination. A vision not only sets the direction but also helps you and your ship's components experience your destination before you get there. This is important because you will be asking the components to do work—to

---

[4] Nathaniel Zinsser, *The Confident Mind: A Battle-Tested Guide to Unshakable Performance* (New York: Custom House, 2022).

take actions that will send your ship into some rough seas. Some sea states will cause breakages; others will force you to change course. Yet you and your ship will keep going in part because you and your ship have been repeatedly envisioning the future destination and you have determined it's worth the work to reach it.

Envisioning Tips

To make the vision as powerful as possible, you want to include not only Technicolor but also as many other senses as possible, such as sound, smell, taste, and touch. Envisioning is the dream-to-vision conversion process, and the point of this conversion is bringing your dream to a reality in your mind.[5] There is science to back up the envisioning process.

When we visualize an action, the same brain regions are stimulated as when we physically perform an action.[6] This is because our brain perceives the envisioned scenario as real, which can lead to actual physical changes. For instance, imagining a movement can change how our brain networks are organized.[7] It's been found that mental practices like visualization can enhance motivation, increase confidence and self-efficacy, improve motor performance, prime

---

[5] Many psychologists call the imagination location in your mind the *mind's eye*, a theoretical place inside your mind where you experience a form of reality based on what you imagined.

[6] Massa Mohamed Ali, "The Science of Visualization: Can Imagining Your Goals Make You More Likely to Accomplish Them?" *Neurovine.AI* (blog), May 24, 2022, https://www.neurovine.ai/blog/the-science-of-visualization-can-imagining-your-goals-make-you-more-likely-to-accomplish-them.

[7] Jim Lohr, "Can Visualizing Your Body Doing Something, Such as Moving Your Arm, Help You Complete the Action? What Part of the Brain Is Involved?," *Scientific American Mind* 26, no. 3 (2015): 72, https://doi.org/10.1038/scientificamericanmind0515-72a.

your brain for success, and even improve memory and immune system functioning.[8, 9]

The more detailed your envisioning, the better. There are tools available for you to create an actual movie of your vision. Dr. Joe Dispenza's work suggests that detail-oriented visualization, or "creating a movie of your vision," can be particularly effective.[10] Other techniques include listening to a certain song while envisioning your outcome. Carl Zimmer's work on evolutionary biology suggests that our ability to envision different future outcomes has been a key factor in our survival and success as a species,[11] reinforcing the potential power of multisensory envisioning techniques.

Vision boards have long been used as a simple way to build out the storyboard of your vision. I find a vision board so helpful for cuing your vision movie that I created a portable one that travels with me, known as the UNSTOPPABLE Vision Board.[12] It's a uniquely designed five-panel, folded, on-the-go vision board that can hold up to five visions and sixteen dreams. You can make the most elaborate "vision movie" you like, but the most critical component of the movie

---

[8] A. J. Adams, "Seeing Is Believing: The Power of Visualization," *Psychology Today* (blog), December 3, 2009, https://www.psychologytoday.com/us/blog/flourish/200912/seeing-is-believing-the-power-visualization.

[9] Srinivasan Pillay, "The Science of Visualization: Maximizing Your Brain's Potential During the Recession," *HuffPost* (blog), November 17, 2011, https://www.huffpost.com/entry/the-science-of-visualizat_b_171340.

[10] Joe Dispenza, *You Are the Placebo: Making Your Mind Matter* (Carlsbad, CA: Hay House Inc., 2014).

[11] Carl Zimmer, *She Has Her Mother's Laugh: The Powers, Perversions, and Potential of Heredity* (New York: Dutton, 2018).

[12] "Unstoppable Vision Board." Be Unstoppable. Accessed September 19, 2023, https://beunstoppable.com/product/unstoppable-vision-board/.

is how often you play it. Repetition helps keep the captain and ship on course for your desired destination. I find that the more I play my vision movie, the more my mind will add creative elements to make it even more enjoyable, which in turn leads to being even more committed to making a new reality.[13]

Reminder: The purpose of envisioning is encoding a new series of commands on your subconscious operating system. As you repeat the envisioning process, you are training your brain to help you seek the actions you imagined in your vision. Envisioning is getting your subconscious (and conscious) to work together to help you figure out how to experience the vision you envision (aka keep driving to your destination!).

Stage Three: Vision to Goal

Once you have crafted your vision, the next two steps are much more methodical. As one of my SEAL instructors would like to say, "It ain't complicated. It's just hard." Perhaps you've heard the old saying "goals are dreams with deadlines." That is definitely one component of the next process: adding a deadline for when you want to achieve your goal gives you a sense of urgency. The other part is deciding how you are going to measure your goal. By measure, I mean adding a unit of measurement to your goal so you can track your progress in the direction of your goal. For example, if your goal is to write a book, then your goal unit of measurement could be words written; a

---

[13] Entire books are written on this subject, and here are a few you will find useful: Dr. Wayne W. Dyer, *Wishes Fulfilled: Mastering the Art of Manifesting* (Carlsbad, CA: Hay House Inc., 2012); Dr. Joe Dispenza, *Becoming Supernatural: How Common People Are Doing the Uncommon* (Carlsbad, CA: Hay House Inc., 2017); Jack Canfield and Peter Chee, *The Power of Visualization* (ITD Publishing, 2011).

weight-loss goal would be tracked in pounds lost; or earning money would be tracked in dollars saved. I appreciate these are easily tracked goals; you will have to get more creative when a goal is more nebulous such as "live overseas" or "make the varsity team" or "build an *Inc.* 500 company." In some cases, you might have to make smaller goals that build up to the bigger goal, but remember, the key factor of making a goal a successful goal is that you can measure your achievement of it. If you can measure your goal, then you can reward your progress, and if you can reward progress, then you will keep trying to achieve it.

Deadline Tips

From 2003 to 2005, I raised $1.5 million from thirty-seven of my closest friends and family members to create and launch the BodyRev, the world's greatest fat-burning device.

My guess is you have not seen or heard of it, and worse, you most likely have no clue how it helps you burn fat (that's another story). More to the point, I had raised enough money to launch the product on TV using infomercials. When the first infomercial didn't work, we pushed our timelines out and tried again, and again, and yet again. Over the course of three and a half years, we learned $1,475,000 worth of ways *not* to launch the product. I decided it was time to switch directions and launch a totally different product. This time, there was a completely different sense of urgency—I had only $25,000 and a team of five people who had grown weary, and perhaps doubtful that we could launch a successful product. I asked everyone to give me ninety days.

If after three months we couldn't make the next product work, then I would shut down the business.

Incidentally, the main selling point to my small team was sharing a vision of success with them. I would often remind them, "Imagine what it will be like when our product becomes the top-selling product in the industry or when we have the number one–ranked infomercial or when we have retailers asking us to please send more product!" Visions are powerful tools, not just for yourself but also for your team members. We all need reminders, and the more powerful and concrete you can make that vision, the more connection you can build to your teammates and help them stay focused on making that vision your collective reality.

Eighty-seven days later, and after many more vision-reminding conversations, we launched this product: the Perfect Pushup.

Have you seen this? More than fifteen million pairs have been sold in the United States alone. This story has many layers of lessons learned, but the key lesson learned was the importance of deadlines and commitments. Without a hard-and-fast deadline, I kept extending the finish line for my goal, so much so that I nearly went broke before I shifted course. Deadlines are important, but so is the commitment you attach to meeting that deadline. Deadlines and commitments go hand in hand.

Deadlines are also important for helping you understand the time required to accomplish your goal. For example, if your goal is to save one million dollars in five years but you only commit to saving $100,000 per year, then your commitment is incongruent with your goal. Either your commitment or goal must change. If you change neither, then you are on course for failure, and before you fail, you will likely do what most people do: give up on the goal. You will generate excuses, determine the goal wasn't "really" what you wanted, and essentially abandon the goal (along with your dream that inspired it).

What's worse is that experiencing that "failure" can cause you to think, *Goals are stupid*, or *Goals don't work for me*, or *I just can't do it*. To me, that is the most dangerous part of giving up on your goal, for it sends a message to your brain that sets you up for future failures. That's what we want to avoid—bringing the past into the present, which impacts the future. Not to worry. This will not happen to you, because you are reading this book!

As you transition from a vision to a goal, a further "deadline tip" is deciding how much time to commit to pursuing it on a daily basis. In the beginning, it probably won't be much, and that's okay. It's better right now to set a low bar of time commitment than a high bar where you struggle to meet it in the first week and then realize you can't keep it up, and so you give up entirely. For reference, when I say "give up," I don't just mean throwing your hands up in the air and saying, "I give up," or, "I quit." I mean the much more insidious form of stopping the pursuit of your goal where you come up with a series of excuses that cause you to skip doing an action toward your goal. Over time, you develop a new habit of not acting because of some reasonably thought-out excuse, and before long, you have decided the goal is not worth pursuing.

I want you to think of a commitment like a promise you make to yourself—the highest form of human contract. Any time you start the process of moving toward a new goal, you are starting the process of building a new habit, and this takes time, so be patient. It not only takes time but also requires sacrifice. You will have to stop doing some things and replace them with actions that move you toward your goal. The more you understand what you must give up in your current routine to establish a new one, the more prepared you will be to succeed at building habits in support of your goal. This brings us to the final and most important stage of turning your dream into reality: daily action.

Stage Four: Goal as Daily Action

You can have the most spectacular dream, develop an insanely detailed vision board and movie, and create an elaborate goal plan, but if you don't take daily action, then none of the planning matters. Taking daily action with your full agency matters most. Now this may sound overly simplistic, but think about any type of achievement—climbing a mountain, writing a book, starting a business, learning a new language, helping a community, inventing a product, winning a championship, or landing the lead role in a play. In every single example, the goal is based on a daily action from taking steps (climbing a mountain), to writing words, to helping people, to sketching ideas, to practicing a sport or lines of a play. Making your dream your reality is based on your ability to take consistent daily action.

The key to taking daily action is dividing your goal into smaller and smaller chunks until you can commit to doing action toward it every day. If you are writing a book, this might mean starting with only writing a hundred words per day, and those hundred words might take you three minutes or thirty minutes. The point is you are developing a new daily habit of committing yourself to the action of writing. You will not always write a hundred words; you will become a better and a more efficient writer over time (repetition is the mother of perfection, and perfect repetition is even better!), and a hundred words per day could very well grow into a thousand words or more.

Repetitive daily actions will strengthen your mindset muscles, and you will find that the more you do it, the longer you can do it for, and the easier it becomes. Your action becomes your habit. Think of daily action like getting a ship underway or an airplane to take flight; there will be a lot of energy spent to initially move, but once underway or airborne, you do not need as much fuel.

In the beginning, you will be guessing at what your best daily action should be, and you may guess incorrectly—do not worry about this. Smile and take pride that you are acting, even when it is not the best action. Maybe your goal is to climb one of the Seven Summits, yet you aren't sure how much time you will be able to commit to training weekly. Start slow with thirty minutes of climbing at a pace you can maintain—your pace and time period are not as important as starting.

What often happens is we allow our focus to shift regarding our goals, and we get overwhelmed by the sheer magnitude of it, such as climbing Denali (20,310 feet, the tallest mountain in North America). Our inner critic (which I call the Whiner) "whines" about why thirty minutes is not nearly enough time to train, therefore we should wait until we have sixty or ninety minutes to devote to it, or even better, "Let's wait until the weekend when you can do two hours of steady state climbing." Meanwhile, you miss the entire week, convincing yourself that training only matters if you do two hours or more. If you fall into this trap, you miss massive opportunities to train throughout the week and build consistency into your training regime. You might cram your steps in on the weekend, but you start to become anxious, and your training feels like fits and starts.

If you are able to override your Whiner, what you will discover is that thirty minutes, which you initially thought was all you could do on a weekday, was pretty easy, and you even found it enjoyable knocking out a thousand-foot stair-stepping workout in a half hour. It was a great way to start your day, and you can do it practically anywhere, such as in hotel stairwells. So, you start to stretch your workouts from thirty to forty-five to sixty minutes over the first month of training. Now your conditioning has improved, and when the weekend comes along your two-hour climbs start getting extended to two and a half hours, then three hours, and before long you are doing four-hour climbs with some serious weight on your back. Your anxiousness turns into excitement for the climb.

Here's how you divide your goal into daily action. First, define the metric that you will use to measure your goal. For example, if you are writing a book, the metric would be "words." A standard 240-page hardcover book is roughly fifty thousand words. Now there's more to writing a book than "just" writing fifty thousand words, such as creating an outline, developing a table of contents, editing, and compiling a bibliography to name a few. But for the sake of simplicity, your goal needs a unit of measure, and words written is the unit of measure.

When you start, think of setting a daily goal like you are trying to get in shape doing a type of physical exercise you have never done before. For instance, let's say you have never rowed before, and you have decided to start rowing. Would you start off by trying to row more than an hour every day? If you tried that the first week, you'd find ways not to go back the next week because your hands would be full of blisters, your back would ache, and your legs would be cramping.

When doing anything new, build up. Start with twenty or thirty minutes, just enough to make some progress but not enough to scare you off. After the first week, look at your goal production. How many words did you write on Monday versus Friday? My guess is your goal production improved as you became more comfortable writing. Then reevaluate your daily action goals weekly. After you complete a week of daily action, decide if you should modify those goals for the next week.

Speaking of taking daily action, I want you to record your daily action on a calendar. Write it down. If you have an assistant, let that person know you aren't reachable during the time you've set aside for your daily action. Put your phone in airplane or do-not-disturb mode and focus on taking your daily action. As you adjust your weekly goals, you can then look at adjusting your bigger goal deadline for completion. But do not race to change your goal's deadline until you have completed at least three weeks of daily action. Habits take a while to form, and I do not want you to lose steam because you hastily decided that, because you had one great week of writing, you should accelerate your book writing deadline only to learn that you cannot keep up that pace. It's better to underpromise and over-deliver to yourself.

I know this movie because I starred in it. And, yes, I have fallen victim to the Whiner before shifting my focus to something I could do every day that I then scaled over time. Mountain-climbing metaphors are great parallels for life: every climb starts with taking a single step. The same is true with a goal: start with a single action, and then keep on going.

COMMON GOAL-SETTING MISTAKES

Goal setting is just the first step in the achievement process, but it is a critical element that can set you up for success or set you on course for frustration and failure. Here are the seven most common reasons why people fail to achieve their goals.

1. **Having no compelling connection to your goal.** When you make a goal, understand why you want it and what you are willing to sacrifice to get it. This book has lots of tools to help you build the proper connections to your goals. Hint: Until the fear of staying put is *greater* than the fear of moving in the direction of your goal, you will stay put.
2. **Setting daily commitments that are too challenging.** As discussed above, ease yourself into taking daily action. Make your initial daily action a simple task that you know you can complete. This will lead you to taking more action day after day and put you on a course for success.
3. **Not measuring progress.** Progress is the fuel of persistence. If you do not make your goal measurable, then you cannot track your progress, and if you cannot track your progress, then you will not achieve your goal. No matter what your goal is, make it measurable. Tracking progress is your secret weapon to goal success.
4. **Losing focus.** There is an entire section of this book on focus—it is one of our key controllables to help us achieve anything. If we lose focus, we lose the ability to take committed action. There are all kinds of ways to lose focus, and there are five great tools to keep your focus, all discussed in chapter seven.
5. **Listening to the wrong people.** This could technically fall under "losing focus," but I want to call this to your attention as its own reason for goal failure: listening to people who have *not* achieved or attempted to achieve what you are trying to achieve. They may not mean you any harm. In fact, they may be trying to help you avoid the pain they endured when they failed to achieve the goal. Be *very* intentional about to whom you decide to listen.

6. **Procrastinating.** We all procrastinate. Why do something today that can be postponed to tomorrow? This way of thinking is a trap that sets you up for long-term failure. If you learn nothing from this book, *please* remember this: taking daily action toward your goal is what matters most.
7. **Taking the wrong actions.** The definition of insanity is taking the same action yet expecting a different result. In this book, I share practices on how to use your failures as fuel to press on. Expect to make mistakes, as doing so is part of the learning process. What we want to avoid is repeating failures by not learning from them.

Personal goals can be about your physical health, your family life, or simply personal to you in some other way, but they must be measurable. Saying, "I want to be happy," is not a measurable goal unless you have a unit of measurement for your happiness. For example, a way to measure your happiness could be to make a goal of doing something on a regular basis that brings you great happiness (e.g., traveling to a foreign country ever year, fishing once a month, coaching your kid's sports teams, taking a weekly walk in nature). The fundamentals here are knowing what brings you happiness and then creating a unit of measurement to gauge how you'll take action on your happiness. The same rules apply for professional goals, and the more specific, the better.

To help you get your creative juices flowing, here are my ten-, three-, and one-year goals.

TEN YEARS

Personal

1. Climb the Seven Summits and ski to the North and South Poles.
2. Take my family on vacations to all seven continents.

Professional

1. Help 1 percent of the US population achieve a goal (roughly 3.5 million people).
2. Build a goal-setting software platform that can scale to processing one billion goals.

THREE YEARS

Personal

1. Ski to the South Pole, climb Aconcagua, and conduct a couple hikes in the Dolomites hut to hut.
2. Take a family trip to Australia and write graduation books for Charlie and John (when my boys graduate from high school, I write them personal books to help inspire them for their future goal pursuits).

Professional

1. Have *Unstoppable Mindset* translated in twenty-five languages and sell one million copies.
2. Help people achieve one hundred thousand goals.

ONE YEAR

Personal

1. Climb Aconcagua and plan the South Pole adventure.
2. Complete Charlie's graduation book.

Professional

1. Design, build, and test the goal software platform.
2. Complete the *Unstoppable Mindset* book and deliver fifty speeches on its content.

Accomplishing goals, especially audacious ones that can transform your life, takes time. This is a marathon, not a sprint, and there will be lots of challenges ahead that I will help you navigate in the coming chapters. But before we turn to chapter two, I want you to perform the goal exercise I shared above. Warning: Take time to think about it. Please write down your ten-, three-, and one-year goals below. I want you to come up with two personal and two professional goals for each time frame. (Swim buddy, that's an order.)

WHAT IS AN UNSTOPPABLE MINDSET?

2 You Are the Captain

When we became engaged in the '90s, I promised my wife that we would live in Europe. I thought that was going to be an easy promise to fulfill because my next duty station was supposed to be in Rota, Spain, working as the operations officer of a Navy SEAL base. Shortly after getting married, I was offered the opportunity to serve a special SEAL Team. As my orders changed, so did my bride's hopes for living in Europe.

In the summer of 2015, I made good on my twenty-year-old promise. I had sold Perfect Fitness to a much larger consumer products company called Implus Corporation, and over my three years with Implus, I rose to president of the fitness division. We had made great strides growing the business through both acquisition and internal product development. We had just successfully sold Implus to another private equity firm. As the deal closed, I made a decision that was completely counterintuitive to a successful career in consumer products: leaving it.

I spent weeks going on long walks thinking about leaving a perfectly great job to move to Spain with our four kids. After lots of walks, a few restless nights, and several hours of financial planning, I resigned (with four months' notice) and prepared for a two-year journey living in Barcelona. I could write several books on living overseas with four high-energy boys (at the time five, seven, nine, and eleven years old). I will save you many of the highs and lows (there were plenty of both) from traveling with a family of six to twenty-five countries and seventy-five cities in two years, but there is one visit in particular that I want to share.

Early in our Spanish adventures, we went to Santiago, a northwestern Spanish town, home to the end of a popular pilgrimage route called El Camino de Santiago. Santiago is a historic town and definitely worth a visit for many reasons from the food to history to being home to the oldest continually operated hotel in the world. But it is also the site of Spain's westernmost point of land. This location is kilometer zero, i.e., where the pilgrimage ends after starting in France. (While there are several "caminos" one can take starting in Spain, France, or Portugal, all end at Finisterra.)

The term *Finisterra* means "end of the world." Over a thousand years ago, the Romans named this western tip of Spain Finis Terrea (Land's End) because, to them, these rolling rocks into the sea outside the town of Santiago marked the end of the earth. They had no reason to explore further. It took more than 1,500 years for explorers to challenge the Romans' belief that the world ended just west of Santiago.

We all have our own "Finisterra" in our minds. We all have preconceptions of our limits. It's normal for us to have them. We both inadvertently and purposely developed them over our lifetimes, and if we do not challenge them, we will find ourselves living lives constrained by them.

Challenging our limits doesn't happen in one large action. We must take lots of smaller actions that over time help us develop confidence in taking bigger steps to redefine our limits. I have front-loaded this book with two chapters on goals because the self-limits we set contribute to the boundaries of our goals. Put another way, as you read the remaining chapters of this book, I want you to test your assumed limits versus your goals. Often when first asked for their ten-, three-, and one-year goals, people make their goals too achievable.

Often, ten-year goals are really somewhere between three- and five-year goals. Three-year goals are closer to one-year goals, and one-year goals are more akin to quarterly goals. Quarterly goals are where SMART Goals should live—goals that are specific, measurable, achievable, realistic, and timely. Too often, people believe that all goals should be SMART Goals. When every goal is made with a realistic timeline, we set ourselves up for underachieving. The point of ten- and three-year goals is to stretch your imagination about what can be done. Use SMART goal setting for those goals you need to accomplish in the short term that build to the longer-term goals.

I have found two leading reasons why people unintentionally lower the bar on what they can achieve. Number one, people are so used to setting bottom-up goals influenced by our financial reporting system (i.e., aversion to failure) of quarterly goals that, over time, they only think about goals in ninety-day increments. Because of that, people stop dreaming audaciously and further into the future. Dreaming is a muscle—it requires practice and will atrophy without consistent exercise. The good news is, dreaming is like riding a bike. You did it as child, and you can do it again as an adult, but you must try.

Spend time daydreaming about what you are going to do with your Unstoppable Mindset once you finish this book. There is an exercise at the end of this book that will require you to reevaluate the goals you outlined at the end of the chapter one. As folks learn the Unstoppable Mindset tools, they open their minds to bigger and bolder goals, and that makes my heart sing! My mission is to help you achieve more than you originally thought was possible. After all, what good is an Unstoppable Mindset if you do not put it to use?

STRETCHING YOUR GOALS

I will never forget the first time I lost sight of land as the captain of a boat. I was a student in the Navy SEAL course called Long-Range over the Horizon Navigation. I was in a fifteen-foot-long inflatable boat with a fifty-five-horsepower outboard. The center of the boat was filled with rubber fuel bladders, forcing us to constantly adjust our positioning so we wouldn't puncture the bladders. Our only navigational tools were a chart and small compass strapped to the portside (left) pontoon. The basic theme of OTH (over-the-horizon) training was simple—learn to navigate small boats over long distances to arrive at exact locations at specific times. (GPS systems were available, but the instructors wanted us to learn how to navigate the old-fashioned way, should our GPS not work, which is not uncommon when you mix saltwater with electronics.)

Our initial courses were simple and relatively short, ranging between ten and twenty nautical miles. (A nautical mile is 2,000 yards, whereas a mile on your car's odometer is 1,760 yards.) These courses were simple because we could aim from one side of San Diego Harbor to the next using landmarks as our navigational aids. The first couple of days were spent crisscrossing San Diego Bay, learning how to stay on course using the boat's compass at different speeds while tracking our progress using a paper chart. We would choose landmarks that we could see from our vantage point, about four feet above the water in calm seas, sitting down in our boat. Landmarks needed to be tall and distinct so the skipper of the craft could focus on them day or night. We would navigate the exact same daytime course at night to experience the difficulty of seeing the same landmarks at night. Water towers, radio antennas, and high-rise apartment buildings became difficult to distinguish from each other once the sun went down.

After a couple of days of getting comfortable learning how to navigate our little motorized vessels both day and night within sight of land, it was time for us to leave the harbor to navigate courses over the horizon. There is this moment when you lose sight of land and you realize that you have lost the comfort of landmarks for reference points. Every direction you turn looks exactly the same. Now not only must you use different navigational tools such as the sun and wave direction, but also the compass is no longer a "nice-to-have" secondary tool but your primary navigational instrument upon which your mission depends. You guard it with your life. Suddenly, everyone in the boat became extra careful with the compass straps. We sat farther away from it and kept anything magnetic as far away from it as possible.

For the next seven days we covered hundreds of miles driving our little boats over the horizon, getting accustomed to navigating with limited tools and without the comfort of landmarks. It is disorienting, and if you allow your focus to drift, it can quickly become terrifying, floating in the ocean in a little boat thinking of how vulnerable you are. However, over time, you learn to trust your compass. You become comfortable with your ability to navigate long distances through rough waters in a boat that has more capabilities than you first realized. So long as you take care of your fuel and engine, you can go much farther than you ever thought was possible in a fifteen-foot inflatable boat. But getting to those realizations is uncomfortable because you must go beyond your original perception of what you thought was possible.

That's the point: going after a dream is much like crossing the horizon. You will find yourself, at some point, losing sight of land and the landmarks that provide you comfort. You will have to shift your focus and learn to depend on a new set of tools, one of which is your own form of a compass (namely, your heart and gut). Your fuel is your personal energy to power you day after day pursuing a course that takes you farther away from the familiarity and comfort of your safe harbor. Your engine is your body taking actions that propel you closer to your destination—your goal.

I speak to thousands of people each year about how to build an Unstoppable Mindset. One of the first topics is comparing the pursuit of a dream with crossing an ocean, and I ask them a question: "Do you know how far you can see if you are a six-foot-tall person standing on the sea on a dead calm day before the horizon blocks your view?"

People shout out, "Twenty-five miles!" or "Fifty kilometers!" I've even heard "A hundred miles!" The point is the horizon is much closer than you think—it's only 2.9 miles away. Yet here's the challenge: your dream is way past the horizon. So far past that you cannot see it with your eyes. You must first "see" it with your mind's eye. The old adage of "seeing is believing" is incorrect. When you start on a course toward making a dream come true, believing becomes your compass, and the old adage turns into a new paradigm where you must first believe in order to see.

There is this point on your metaphorical over-the-horizon navigation course to make your dream a reality when you lose sight of land. This point is an inflection point on your course.

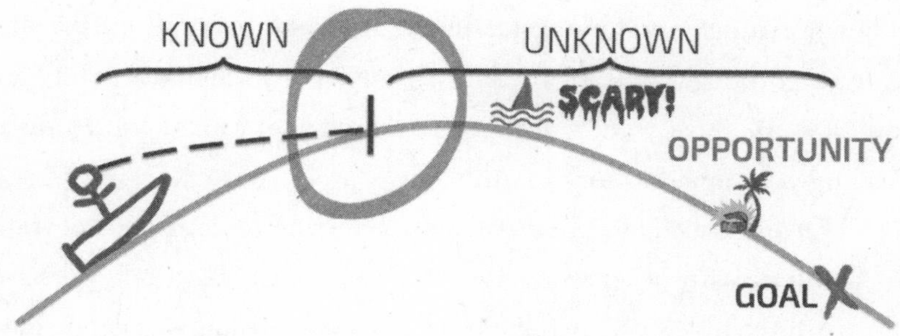

When you shift from the comfort zone of familiarity to the uncomfortable zone of the unknown, you shift from seeing to believing. The circle denotes this imaginary line of mindset demarcation where our resolve is put to the test. It is here that we must make a decision between *can* and *can't*. Your mindset comes down to this simple yet difficult decision of whether something *can* or *can't* be done—you can press on or quit. I think of this decision-making process like the game show *Wheel of Fortune*, except instead of dollars and bankruptcy opportunities, we are constantly "spinning" to decide if we can achieve our goals.

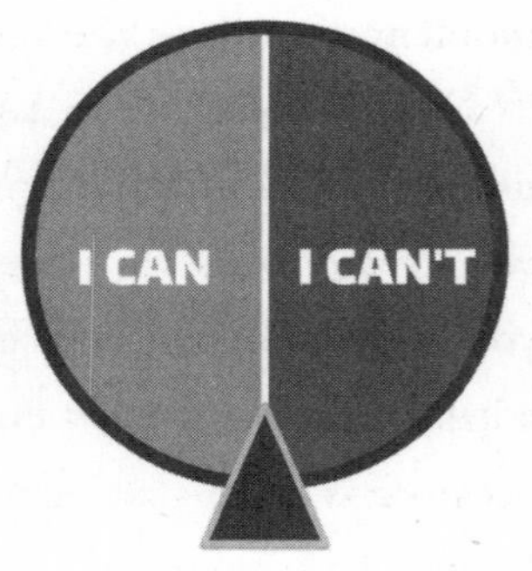

NAVIGATIONAL CHALLENGES AND HAZARDS

Going after a new goal is similar to crossing a new ocean. It can feel terrifying and lonely. The journey can fill you with doubt, leaving you questioning your new course. It can shake your confidence and convince you that your dream is nothing more than a foolish folly, leading you to turn around. There are three major moments to be aware of when pursuing your dream: starting, failing, and tiring (thinking you cannot go on). I think of these as major navigational waypoints (or milestones), and I want you to be aware of them as you contemplate leaving your own harbor of familiarity.

When I use the term *harbor*, I am referring to your current state of familiarity. In other words, your comfort zone. It's a natural state for us to seek pleasure and avoid pain. In everything we do, we naturally seek comfort. The comfort zone is not a bad place unless it holds us back from realizing our full potential. It is key to recognize when we have reached a level of comfort or familiarity or mastery in a particular skill. If we are not careful, we allow ourselves to get lulled into a false sense of security and believe we are good enough, and stop plotting course to new ports.

Like ships built to be at sea, we are built to be in motion. The moment we stop is the moment our systems start to rust. In SEAL Team, we often refer to a skill as a "perishable skill." Simply put, use it or lose it. This tenet of practice is critical to your success. The more you work toward your goal, the better you'll become, and the closer you will get to achieving it. That's why the first challenge is building a habit of doing the work daily toward your dream. The path to every dream has these three detours (starting, failing, and tiring) waiting for you. In keeping with our ship's metaphor, I think of them like this: leaving the harbor, losing sight of land, and dealing with darkness.

Leaving the Harbor

When people hear I was "the Navy SEAL who invented the Perfect Pushup," I often hear, "Wow, what an overnight success!" The fact is I did not invent the Perfect Pushup alone (there were about ten people involved), and it was an overnight success that took nearly ten years. I did not start my entrepreneurial fitness journey thinking that we would be running infomercials selling handheld fitness devices (my team also invented the Perfect Pullup, Perfect Situp, and the Perfect Ab Carver), but I did start it knowing I wanted to launch products that would help people take control of their bodies and, in doing so, would in some way help them take control of their lives.

In the beginning, my starting point was carving out thirty minutes of time after dinner each night to sketch product ideas. Each night as I sat down at our kitchen table in our studio apartment in San Francisco, I thought about making a little progress toward my faraway destination of being an *Inc.* 500 CEO/founder who created a company based on ideas that helped other people. I wanted the experience of creating a new-to-the-world product and bringing it to market. That was my original goal, and my daily action was sketching each night until I had come up with an idea that I could take to a draftsman/designer who could help bring my drawings to life. I figured that once I had some professional drawings, I might attract investors, a manufacturer, and, hopefully, a partner. It took me over a year to "leave the harbor" and get that first idea sketched out so others could get an understanding of what was bouncing around in my head.

I call this initial phase *leaving the harbor* because it's hard to embark on a journey in the direction of an unknown destination. You find yourself battling your own doubts constantly. I can remember nightly discussions with my inner naysayers—*You draw like s---. Why do you think you can create something that hasn't been created before? You don't have any training to invent a product.* Every night, these and many more negative thoughts raced through my head before I even got up from the sofa and walked the five steps to the kitchen table to open my drawing journal and start.

Pushing past these doubts to leave the harbor is the first critical phase of developing an Unstoppable Mindset, and it often stops many of us because we convince ourselves we aren't ready, or not worthy, or not capable of even starting our new adventure. I am here to tell you that is all just a mental trap to keep us "safe," anchored in the harbor of familiarity. Our brains do not want to work harder than they have to. They are constantly seeking the path of least resistance. When you find yourself taking initial action toward your new course and these voices start barking at you in your brain, you can smile, because you are leaving the harbor of mediocrity and setting a course toward something new and exciting!

Losing Sight of Land

"Go away!" yelled the man I had driven six hours to see. Before I could respond, he followed with, "I'm done working with inventors. I have a drawer full of my own ideas to work on." The man barking at me was world-class designer Stephen G. Hauser. He and his team of designers had helped bring to market over seven hundred products, from medical devices to business machines and more. His design studio was known around the world for designing the best products, and I wanted him to help us design our fitness product. I had driven from San Francisco to Los Angeles in my VW with twenty pounds of modeling clay piled on my wife's cutting board. The clay, which was poorly molded and already cracking from the heat in the trunk, represented my best attempt to showcase the fitness idea bouncing around in my head.

I persisted, telling him I had driven down from the Bay Area so I could spend ten minutes with him. "Sir, would you just give me ten minutes to show you my idea?"

He looked at me like he had just seen a ghost, and asked, "Did you just call me 'sir'?"

"Yes, I did, sir."

His demeanor changed, and he suddenly became curious. "What's your background? I mean what have you done in your life?"

"My first job was serving in the Navy, sir."

He looked at me, eyes wide, and smiled as he said, "The Navy saved my life. I'll give you ten minutes but not a second more."

That was the beginning of a glorious friendship that continues to this day. Steve Hauser, at the time of our meeting, was one of only fifty Industrial Design Society of America Fellows. He is a living legend in the world of industrial design, and he taught me the basics of taking an idea from a napkin to production.

His first rule is: prepare to fail—a lot. (Another key rule is don't get attached to your initial idea, which I learned the hard way—more on that later.) Whether you are trying to bring a product to market or you are trying out for a new team, mistakes are part of the process. The challenge becomes not letting the mistakes define you. Once you get started and you have left your proverbial harbor and headed over the horizon toward your dream, prepare to embrace failure.

As you pick up steam and start making consistent progress toward your goal, you will face failure. I think of this obstacle like losing sight of land in your little boat, where you may feel all alone, and even frightened, as challenges start coming at you from every direction. Speaking of direction, you can get quickly confused about the direction you should be traveling. I drove down to see Mr. Hauser confident that I had a specific product direction. By the time he finished asking me questions, my head was spinning with possibilities that left me questioning my original direction. After we nailed down the features and functions for our product, we started prototyping. I was convinced that we would only have to do one prototype. Boy, was I wrong! Two years later and after probably twenty different product variants, we finally had a product (BodyRev) we could bring to market.

Over a three-and-half-year period, I failed so many times that I lost count. As a matter of fact, I remember asking our small team, "Okay, what's our failure of the week this week?" We started joking about how many different things we would fail at. This is an extreme example of failing, perhaps not as extreme as Thomas Edison's "I learned ten thousand ways not to make a light bulb" story, but for me, it was the most failing I had ever experienced, and I was no stranger to failing. I have failed at lots of different things from classes at the Naval Academy to failing pool competency at Basic Underwater Demolition/SEAL (BUD/S) (twice) to failing in graduate school, in business, as a husband, father, and as a leader of charitable organizations. However, and I really stress *however*, I do not let failing stop me. I will pivot, tack, veer, turn, switch, change direction, and give blood, but I do *not* let failing hold me back. This is doubt's second trap, to convince you after you failed a few times that your dream is not possible or worth pursuing. It is doubt's trap to trick you into losing your belief and, hence, your goal and focus.

I will arm with some powerful weapons to help you transform failing into fuel for your persistence engines. As a matter of fact, be more concerned if you are not failing because that means you aren't pushing hard enough. For example, every time we bring a new product to market, we figure out how to break it. When I write a book, I write thousands (as in tens of thousands) more words than I know will make the cut; when I come up with a new product idea, I immediately think of all the ways it can fail. Succeeding is based on learning from failing. You need the strength from the struggle of failure to help you reach the horizon of success.

Experts fail more than amateurs try.

Enough said.

Darkest Before Dawn

Nearly four years after Stephen Hauser developed our product and we had raised $1.5 million, we found ourselves with less than $25,000 left. We were broke. We did not have enough money to pay the manufacturer, our accountant, or even our lawyers. Some of our investors said the only path forward was bankruptcy. We had worked for almost four years on a product that clearly was not working. Every "expert" seemed to say the same thing: "You are out of money—go bankrupt and get a job." It was a truly dark moment, and the more we focused on how dark it was, the darker it got for us. I knew from my days in SEAL training that the more we focused on the negative, the more negative our thinking would become, and I also knew that many times the darkest of times means that dawn is just around the corner. I think of it like flipping on a mental light switch—a switch that illuminates possibilities. Whether you are out at sea or deep down your path to accomplishing your dream, finding yourself stuck in darkness and feeling surrounded by hopelessness is a key phase of the journey.

Flipping that mental switch is hard, and is in part why I wrote this book. I want to teach you how to flip that switch, because when your proverbial darkness occurs while pursuing your dream, it can become very easy to focus on your pain and suffering in that moment. I am using "darkest before dawn" as a metaphor for the third obstacle in your mental journey to find success. How many times have you heard the story of someone trying and trying and then giving up, only to discover they were so close to their goal?

There will come this moment when you start shifting your focus to the pain of trying and failing, trying and not making progress, or trying and finding the pursuit getting harder. You might begin questioning yourself, wondering, *How much more can I handle?* That's the darkness creeping in, and it brings doubt along with it. Doubt will get you thinking you have run out of steam and that you can't keep going. In David Goggins's book *Can't Break Me*, the former SEAL theorizes that on average the moment you think you can't go any farther means you're only around 40 percent spent, meaning you have another 60 percent to go. Once you break through that limitation, you will discover that it was nothing more than your own glass ceiling. You will realize this is your "darkest before dawn" moment. It will not stop you—instead, it will fuel you to press on.

When you learn to overcome this final hurdle, you will discover that the subsequent journeys will become easier because you will not fall victim to doubt when you are starting, failing, or tiring. The first technique to conquering these obstacles is being aware of them. As you learn to harness the power of your focus with this book, you will be able to put these obstacles in perspective, deprive them of attention (i.e., energy), and keep your focus on taking the actions required to succeed.

I am a visual learner. The moment I learn a new concept, I immediately think of it in detailed pictures. When it comes to thinking about these obstacles and pursuing dreams, I map them to crossing the horizon. Using the same horizon illustration from earlier in this chapter, here is how I map the three obstacles that we all face when embarking on achieving something new to us.

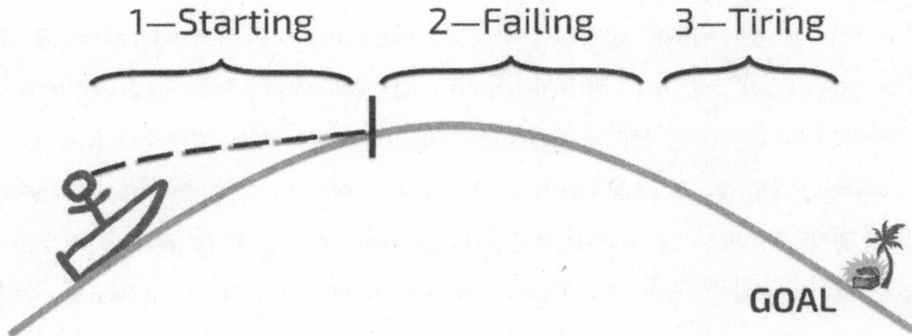

1. **Starting.** The biggest challenge is just showing up. Mark Twain's insight is as true today as it was over a hundred years ago: "The secret of getting ahead is getting started." Woulda/shoulda/couldas show up at the start and prevent so many from even trying to go after their dreams. The key action is taking the first step.
2. **Failing.** Once you leave the harbor and encounter the rough seas in uncharted waters, sticking to your course can be difficult, while changing course as you learn new skills is to be expected. Failing tests your resolve and makes you stronger and smarter (as long you use your failures as learning opportunities!).
3. **Tiring.** We are human, and we all need to recharge. Feeling like we have run out of steam happens to everyone as they are persisting. Keep "tiring" in perspective and use those moments to recharge, take a break, or fuel up. Oftentimes the best fuel comes from reviewing your progress even if your progress is a series of lessons learned from failing.

FUEL OR ANCHOR—IT'S YOUR CALL

To overcome these three mindset obstacles and cross your metaphorical ocean to reach your new desired destination (achieve your goal), you must activate a series of your ship's components that will act as either fuel to propel you forward or anchor to hold you back. Each of us has these components. The reason not all of us use them is because they require us to make a series of decisions each and every day to use them. This decision is the single most important leadership role you have: leading yourself and your three mindset controllables that are the difference makers in your success. These controllables are thoughts, focus, and beliefs. There are very few things we can control in life, but the few things we can control are enough to change our course. This entire book is about helping you harness the power of these controllables to activate your potential to turn your dreams into your new reality.

Our thoughts, focus, and beliefs influence each other to drive us to take actions that will determine our direction. Think of them interacting in a loop—what I call a Mindset Loop. Our thoughts, focus, and beliefs can lift us up and fill us with hope, or they can push us down into the depths of despair where hopelessness lives. Yet they are ours to control, and control them we must if we want to cross the horizon to our new dream destination.

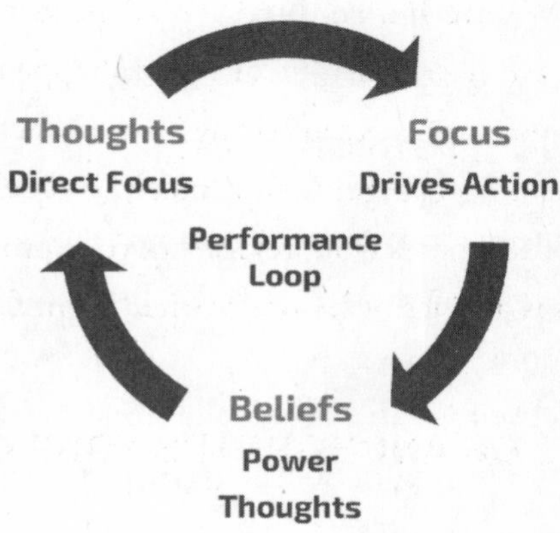

Your three controllables interact with each other as depicted above. Thoughts direct your focus, focus drives an action, and beliefs power your thoughts. It doesn't matter where you enter the loop. Allow your focus to shift from positive to negative, and it will impact what you believe, which in turn will produce corresponding negative thoughts to keep your focus on fueling more negativity. Your Mindset Loop can start with a belief you have carried with you for years, a belief that acts like an anchor that keeps you stuck in the muck of the harbor of mediocrity. Your thoughts and focus remain anchored to that limiting belief until you cut yourself free from it.

Conversely, your thoughts can change your Mindset Loop's focus and replace an old limiting belief, such as "it can't be achieved," with a new, empowering one, such as "we can do this." Each component of the Mindset Loop has its own energy and will influence the other. Momentum builds in either a helpful or hurtful direction toward your goal. For the purposes of teaching you how to make your Mindset Loop an unstoppable force for achieving your goals, I organized the following chapters to follow the Mindset Loop in a clockwise fashion starting with thoughts, then focus, and ending with beliefs, and I will describe how they all work together.

EXERCISE | **Reflection**

Think of a time when you decided to give up. Perhaps it was a time when you gave up before even starting because you decided you couldn't do it or it wasn't possible. Perhaps it was after you had failed a few times and decided it couldn't be done, or perhaps it was after a long period of trying, and you just ran out of steam.

Step 1. Identify the moment—put yourself back in time when you made the decision to quit.

____

____

____

____

Step 2. What were you thinking at that moment? What thoughts did you focus on? What happened when you focused on more of the same kind of thought? Did you find yourself reinforcing those thoughts with a belief?

____

____

____

____

Step 3. How would your life have been different if you had succeeded?

____

____

____

____

We all have these moments in our lives. The point of this reflection is to bring awareness to the thoughts, focus, and beliefs that have sabotaged your success in the past. Soon you will have weapons to slay these dragons in the future.

3
Mindsetting

After four years, I finally stood before the "Creature" at the BUD/S training in Coronado, California. A relic from the 1950s horror film *The Creature from the Black Lagoon*, it was modified with a frogman web belt and a wooden plaque saying, "So You Wanna Be a Frogman." The term *frogman* is a World War II term for what a Navy SEAL is today. SEAL is an acronym that refers to the three environments we operate in: sea, air, and land.

On average, it takes two years to actually see the Creature, if you enlist in the Navy and attend basic boot camp. SEAL candidates must pass several tests, including a physical fitness test (PFT), which they take at least three times before starting BUD/S. Upon arrival at BUD/S, instructors administer the PFT again.

After passing the PFT, candidates enter a seven-week pre-phase training group called fourth phase, where they learn SEAL basics and receive special attention from instructors, such as how to be a sugar cookie (wet and sandy for long periods of time). At the end of our seventh week, we gathered in front of the Creature before taking the PFT one more time.

As we stood silently in formation, the senior instructor of first phase, nicknamed Instructor Half Butt due to a Vietnam tour injury, walked out of his office and stopped in front of the Creature. He loved to remind us that he could do more with his half butt than we could with our full ones. He stood before us, scanning our formation and speaking softly with a southern accent. "Candidates of Class 181, y'all interested in the secret to making it through Navy SEAL training?"

All 122 of us nodded yes simultaneously.

"Then break ranks and gather around," he said quietly.

We huddled eagerly in front of the Creature, anticipating the secret to success in BUD/S.

"The secret ain't complicated," he explained, raising his index finger. "It's just *hard*, 'cause ya just gotta decide what ya gonna focus on—the pain of training or the pleasure it can provide."

He waited for a moment as he let his comments settle in and then said, "I know for a fact that over 80 percent of you are gonna focus on the pain of training. You know why?" He waited again. "Because y'all been focusing on being a SEAL on a sunny day, and that's the rub. Ya see, your country doesn't need SEALs on sunny days—she needs them on scary days, when it's cold, dark, wet." He paused for a moment. "And that crack over ya head, well, that ain't thunder. That's someone who wants ya dead. How bad ya'll want to be a SEAL on that day?"

We exchanged nervous glances and mumbled words of encouragement.

He waited for another moment as he watched our feeble responses to his rhetorical question. "You know what my job is? It's to create a conversation in here"—he raised his right index finger to his temple—"a conversation that will drive you to make a decision about what you are going to focus on: the pain or the pleasure of training."

He went on for a little while longer discussing how he would treat us like the making of a samurai sword, where the swordsmith heats up the metal, pounds on it, and then submerges it in cold water, and repeats that process about two thousand times. He urged us to reflect on our reasons for being here and what we were willing to give. After his speech, we took our final PFT test to qualify for SEAL training. Only sixty-four of us passed; nearly 50 percent failed. Despite having passed the test multiple times before, those who failed had listened to the wrong voice.

THE CONVERSATION OF TWO COMPETING VOICES

Mixed emotions filled the air as our SEAL instructor read out the class-up list of SEAL candidates who qualified to start official SEAL training on Monday. We had bonded over seven weeks of beach runs, physical training, obstacle courses, swimming, and room inspections. A few injuries had occurred, but no had one technically dropped out by ringing the bell.

However, fifty-eight classmates effectively quit by failing to pass the PFT. Their reactions ranged from excuses such as "just not my day" or "I wasn't feeling it" to some admitting they no longer wanted it.

Instructor Half Butt emphasized the importance of "the conversation"—the internal struggle between believing we can or cannot achieve something. This dialogue was crucial in deciding whether to commit to the challenges of SEAL training and the sacrifices required to reach our goals. He made it clear that success wasn't complicated; it was simply hard.

Years later, I named the two voices in this conversation the Whiner and the Winner. Regardless of the situation, these voices arise in us when we attempt something new or challenging. If we are not careful, we will allow the Whiner to initiate a chain reaction within our Mindset Loop where negative thoughts will influence our focus and reinforce negative beliefs that will doom our ability to take successful actions toward our goal. Remember that our thoughts, focus, and beliefs determine our direction. The challenge lies in overcoming the Whiner's fear-driven arguments against pursuing our dreams, which are full of uncertainty and require sacrifice. Learning to take charge of these voices is what I call *mindsetting*—an active management of owning the necessary thoughts that positively influence our focus and beliefs to help us succeed. This is the first crucial lesson in building an Unstoppable Mindset. This chapter is all about helping you identify the various voices of the Whiner and the Winner and how to embrace them to help you overcome obstacles on your course to success.

THE WHINER

You know that high-pitched tone a child uses to complain about something, such as, "Why do I have to eat my vegetables?" "Why do I have to clean my room?" "Why do I have to go to school today?" or a similar tone used when stating their unwillingness to perform a task such as, "I don't want to go," "I don't want to do it"? You know that voice—the one that makes you wince when you hear it. That's the voice I think of in my head when thinking about making a decision that will require me to expend energy doing something where the outcome is unknown. This is the voice of the Whiner.

The Whiner has several tools at its disposal. I think of these tools as different types of voices, and call them the Doubter, the Complainer, the Procrastinator, the Hypothesizer, and the Quitter.

The Doubter

The Doubter often appears when attempting new challenges, aiming to prevent us from taking the starting actions with thoughts such as, "do you know how hard this is going to be?," "why do you think you can do this?," "you're not good enough," or "you have no chance." By making progress and building confidence, we can silence the Whiner. Sometimes the Doubter voice doesn't come from within but from people around us. I often heard, "Alden, you are kidding yourself—you don't have enough experience," or "you're gonna get crushed," or "you have snowball's chance in hell of making it."

When I decided to try out for the prestigious Kent School Boat Club (KSBC) rowing team in high school, my friends were skeptical. Given my limited experience and the fierce competition I'd face, securing a spot on the team seemed impossible. However, I resolved to try and became selective about who I spent time with, avoiding those who amplified the Whiner's voice.

Months before the official tryouts, I consistently trained at the boathouse, facing the Doubter's voice every day. Despite the mental struggle, I persisted, and the doubt diminished as I developed a daily workout habit.

A senior, Charlie Pruesse, noticed my dedication and invited me to be his workout partner. This partnership boosted my confidence, enabling me to push myself harder and subdue the Whiner's doubt. Though the Doubter lingered, working out with someone as positive as Charlie helped me take significant strides toward overcoming my inner obstacles.

The Complainer

We all possess the voice of a Complainer that amplifies our doubts when facing uncertainty. It screeches as we leave our comfort zones, urging us to revert to familiarity and conserve energy. Fueled by negativity bias, the Complainer's primary goal is to keep us safe from potential harm.

Thoughts like *This is harder than I thought*, or *I'm not good at this*, are just a few examples of the Complainer's influence. When we repeatedly fail despite our best efforts, the Complainer emerges, harshly criticizing every misstep: "you suck at this," "who are you kidding?," or "get real; you shouldn't be here." (We often speak to ourselves more severely than what we would tolerate from others.)

Discard those condescending thoughts. They're merely the complaints of the Whiner, magnifying your struggles while learning something new. Remember, it's natural to face difficulties when developing new skills—our brains need frustration to form new neural pathways. So, when the Complainer starts nagging, smile and embrace the challenge, knowing you're on the path to growth and success.

The Procrastinator

"What's your book going to be about, honey?" my wife, Jennifer, inquired as she gently caressed her basketball-sized belly.

"I'm going to write a book to celebrate the birth of our first child—it will be a collection of lessons I've learned while pursuing my dreams," I declared with pride as we sat at the dinner table, discussing our goals for 2003 on New Year's Eve, 2002.

Fast-forward four children and ten years, and the book I had envisioned was finally published on November 14, 2013. In that time, I had become exceptionally skilled at procrastination, and quite frankly, if it hadn't been for my desire to change careers, I'm not sure I would have ever written that book. The Whiner has a sly and sinister voice that excels at encouraging us to procrastinate at taking an action or at committing with our full agency. I hear this voice almost every morning when my alarm goes off, saying: "you don't have to work out this morning; you can do it in the afternoon," or "take a rest and watch the game; you can write extra tomorrow," or "what's the rush?" Don't be deceived by this voice or by "friends" who persuade you to adopt the mindset of *Why do today what you can put off until tomorrow?* It's not the act of procrastinating itself that hinders you; rather, it's the failure to form a habit of taking new daily actions that ultimately prevents you from achieving your dreams.

The Hypothesizer

The Whiner's main weapon is negativity, which has a potent impact on our mindsets. It takes three positive comments to counteract one negative comment. Consider how negative narratives can be compared to launching a product on Amazon, where it takes multiple five-star reviews to offset a single one-star review; get too many one-star reviews and your product is destined not to sell. Similarly, pursuing a dream is like launching a product—too many negative thoughts (think of them as one-star reviews) can lead to abandoning your goals.

The Whiner uses negative hypotheticals to amplify negativity or a negative outcome and focus your mind on future hardships. In SEAL training, instructors use negative hypotheticals to encourage quitting. They will discuss a future final physical test like drownproofing, where you must swim three hundred yards with your hands tied behind your back and your feet bound together. They will then call out your inability to swim well and ask questions such as, "Sir, how do you honestly believe you will pass drownproofing if you barely passed the regular swim test?" Using logic based on some past result, they will get you thinking negatively about something in the future. Focus on that long enough, and you will hypothesize that you should not even try because your situation is hopeless. That is the danger of the Hypothesizer, creating a negative narrative about something in the future that compels you to quit before you ever begin. While the stakes aren't always as high as quitting something outright, negative hypotheticals can gradually plant seeds of doubt in our minds, either stopping us before we begin or eroding our determination to persevere.

The Quitter

"Midshipman Mills, to save us both time and pain, I've prepared this document for you," said my new Naval Academy company officer, handing me my separation papers.

His beady eyes, magnified by thick glasses, stared at me intensely as he continued, "This isn't the school for you. Your record shows max demerits for a senior, yet you have two years left. One more infraction and you're out—which will likely occur within two weeks. I've had successful sea tours and plan to win the color company here. Your performance won't be tolerated, and I'll actively seek your expulsion."

Tempted to quit but determined not to give in, I replied, "No, sir. I'm not signing it."

That conversation still reminds me of the temptation to quit. Many of us have experienced similar moments—we or another naysayer use reasoning that appeals to our sensible selves, suggesting we can't do something and that quitting is no big deal. But don't be fooled—this is the voice of the Whiner's secret agent, the Quitter.

Recognize that voice, then shift your attention to the Winner inside you. You might initially take ineffective or wrong actions, but use those lessons to try again. Don't quit. Don't let external voices or your inner Whiner convince you to give up on your dream. Embrace the challenges and continue pursuing your goals, knowing that every obstacle is an opportunity to learn and grow stronger.

THE WINNER

If the Whiner were a person, it would be a younger version of me, while the Winner is an older, wiser me who is calm and reassuring. My first experience with the Winner was during my sophomore year in high school at spring training for the rowing team. After months of workouts with my senior mentor, Charlie, I made the Kent School Boat Club spring training trip. We rowed twice daily for ten days to determine our boat positions.

I had never experienced varsity-level rowing before, and within a week, my hands were severely blistered from the wooden oars. I developed a fever due to the infections and was sent to a local medical clinic. The nurse cleaned my wounds, taped them up, and gave me antibiotics, advising I take a week of rest. Knowing this would cost me my spot on the team, I decided to continue rowing.

Assistant Coach Eric Houston informed me that I'd be seat racing that afternoon—a brutal competition determining my position on the team. As I grappled with the pain and doubt, Charlie encouraged me, saying, "Alden, time to make all those winter days training in the boathouse count." No one had ever confronted me with such brutal honesty about my situation and its consequences. It was all up to me. I thought back to our winter workouts in the boathouse basement, challenging each other in "bucket" workouts until we puked.

Now, my decision to row or not would determine the outcome of all those hours of training.

My hands were infected, swollen, and oozing pus. I knew people would understand if I didn't row. I asked myself, *How can I row with these hands?* I realized the clawlike position they'd taken being wrapped in bandages was similar to the position they were in when holding an oar. So I called Charlie for help, and he taped my hands into rowing claws.

At practice, the assistant coach looked skeptical, but let me row anyway. The initial strokes hurt, but my hands eventually went numb. After an hour of drills, we began seat races. My hands worsened with each race, the tape unraveling and exposing raw flesh. Finally, it was my turn to race for the bow seat.

As I swapped seats with Tris Coburn, whom I was racing against, he grimaced at my oar for it was coated in blood and puss. The rough wood and salty sweat intensified my pain. Each stroke felt worse than the last, and I questioned if I could continue. In the middle of the race, a tugboat's wake drenched us, soaking my hands and filling both boats with water. Our coach yelled, "Weigh enough!"—rowing slang for "Stop"—and as if on cue, burning pain shot up my arms. It was so intense that I bit my bottom lip to hold back making a sound of anguish.

We spent a couple of minutes bailing water out of the boats in preparation for continuing the remaining two minutes of the seat race. It was during those moments when I heard the Winner voice—it was a soft, firm voice urging me on, reminding me of Charlie's encouragement: "Pain is temporary. Pride lasts forever" (a favorite quotation of his). The more intently I focused on that empowering voice, the more can-do thoughts surfaced. I started mumbling to myself, "Alden, you got this," again and again. Just saying it kept my mind off the pain at that moment. As the race started again, I was overwhelmed by pain, tears began to flow, but I rationalized, *No one can tell I'm crying—I'm soaking wet. So go ahead. Cry all you want!* An energetic surge swelled within me as I started embracing the discomfort, transforming it into a source of joy. My mindset shifted from dreading each stroke to eagerly anticipating the next one. *How much more can I make it hurt?* I challenged myself. *Come on—I want more!* I could hear another favorite saying of Charlie's: "Pain is weakness leaving the body!" I sought ways to turn the pain into pleasure. The more I tuned in to the encouraging voice, the more the discouraging one faded. Soon, I found myself smiling through my tears—an odd sensation. Despite the pain, I was enjoying the experience and winning the race. Moments later, the race ended, and I had earned my seat while uncovering a powerful force within myself. Unbeknownst to me, I was practicing mindsetting during the race. I was, second by second, actively seeking out thoughts that were helpful to the success I was seeking—in this case, to pull as hard I could on that oar while trying to earn my seat on the team.

My empowering voice was the Winner. This voice is often difficult to hear because the Whiner, fueled by fear, is so obnoxiously loud. The Whiner bombards you with all its various voices of fear. However, the Winner's driving force—the emotion of love—can overcome the Whiner but it requires your awareness of the stakes at the moment. The Whiner seeks immediacy of the moment such as "stop the pain," "avoid extra effort," "take the easy path." The Winner is focused on the longer-term pleasure of what the moment might provide you. It is important to understand the power source of these two competing voices: fear and love. The Whiner is grounded by fear while the Winner is fueled by love. In this chapter, I've outlined five different fear-driven voices; there are probably more. For me, making light of these voices helps me accept them for what they are and move beyond them. Over the past forty years, I've identified two key expressions of love for the Winner voice: passion and purpose. By the end of this chapter, you will be able to distinguish between the elemental voices that are trying to stop you and those that are helping you succeed. This is mindsetting.

I like to think of these two elements as the oars on either side of your personal boat. If you have only one oar in the water, you'll find yourself going in circles. But once both oars are engaged, you'll make forward progress. For the sake of discussion, imagine passion as the port oar (left side) and purpose as the starboard oar (right side). It doesn't matter which comes first; both are essential to overcoming any obstacle that fear throws your way. Whether you find passion in your purpose or purpose in your passion, these two forces can propel you past all of fear's manifestations.

Winning with Passion

I've always been drawn to water. Perhaps it's from my childhood summers spent on a small New England lake and Cape Cod, or maybe it's the weightlessness while swimming or the mystery of diving into the unknown. Regardless, I was always eager to try water-related activities. My passion for rowing began when I first saw eight-oared shells racing down the Housatonic River in Kent, Connecticut. Instantly, I felt a connection and knew it was my sport.

I often reference that rowing experience during Florida tryouts when taking risks in new directions. It was the boldest move I had ever made up to that point in my life, and I still feel that whispering passion inside me today. It felt like an inner voice guiding me. People often say, "Trust your gut," or "Follow your heart," but tuning in to that frequency can be difficult with our minds constantly chattering.

Recent neuroscience research has taught us that our brains have roughly eighty billion neurons that are responsible for processing thoughts and sending signals to our body to take action.[1] Interestingly, our hearts and guts also have neurons—approximately 200–600 million and 40,000, respectively.[2, 3] These neurons help us make decisions by transmitting different types of communication: logic from the brain, emotions from the heart, and desires/instincts from the gut.[4] The heart and gut have roles to play.

Making decisions while considering all three intelligence centers leads to being in alignment or achieving congruency. When we allow our thoughts to dominate, we may make compromised decisions that lead to regret. Most regrets arise from our brains, hearts, and guts being out of alignment. To make better decisions, tune in to both the heart's passion and the gut's purpose to capture both emotion and desire. For example, imagine you want to become a Navy SEAL.

---

[1] Suzana Herculano-Houzel, "The Human Brain in Numbers: A Linearly Scaled-Up Primate Brain," *Frontiers in Human Neuroscience* 3 (2009), https://doi.org/10.3389/neuro.09.031.2009.

[2] J. Andrew Armour, "Potential Clinical Relevance of the 'Little Brain' on the Mammalian Heart," *Experimental Physiology* 93, no. 2 (2008): 165–76, https://doi.org/10.1113/expphysiol.2007.041178.

[3] John B. Furness, "Types of Neurons in the Enteric Nervous System," *Journal of the Autonomic Nervous System* 81, no. 1–3 (2000): 87–96, https://doi.org/10.1016/s0165-1838(00)00127-2.

[4] Erik Mayer, "Gut Feelings: The Emerging Biology of Gut–Brain Communication," *Nature Reviews Neuroscience* 12, no. 8 (2011): 453–66, https://doi.org/10.1038/nrn3071.

Your mind acknowledges the physical fitness standards needed for the SEAL test, and you think, *I can do that*. However, your heart dislikes water, and your gut fears combat. Then your ego, the brain's troublesome teammate, tempts you with the idea of being a "badass" SEAL. It's essential to remember that your ego is not your amigo, as it drives shortsighted decisions misaligned with your values. The ego seeks immediate gratification and can entice you to break rules or cut corners.

When the Whiner and its partner, ego, control decision-making, they override your heart and gut signals. Alternatively, problems arise when you let your gut or heart solely guide your choices. The key is to listen to all three intelligent centers: mind, heart, and gut. My mentor J. D. Messinger compares the signals of your heart and gut to the feelings of lightness or heaviness. He will say, "Light is right," meaning if you have lightness around a decision, that's your heart and gut's way of communicating you are on the correct path. Conversely, if you feel a pit in your stomach or a heaviness in your chest—it's your abdomen's way of saying, *Warning!* Understanding your three intelligence centers' signals and what they represent is crucial in learning to lead the internal conversation.

Winning with Purpose

During the fall of my senior year at the Naval Academy, I was on my way to a computer science class when I encountered the senior Navy SEAL at the Academy. LCDR Tough Guy (not his real name) had an out-of-regulation mustache that extended well beyond the corners of his mouth. His chest was adorned with so many ribbons that the Navy SEAL trident was partially obscured by the lapel of his service dress uniform jacket—a black double-breasted blazer. I had only met him briefly before. He stopped me and asked, "Hey, Midshipman Mills, are you going to the SEAL Team tryouts?"

I glanced at him and replied, "I've been thinking about it."

With a deadpan expression, he asked, "Have you ever been bullied before?"

Puzzled, I thought for a moment and said, "Yes, there was this one time—"

He interrupted me, raising his hand. "I didn't ask for the story. SEALs go around the world and stand up to bullies. If that interests you, come to the tryout."

Truth be told, I was intrigued by the idea of joining the SEAL Team, but not for the reason he mentioned. I was drawn to two aspects of the SEAL Team: its emphasis on water-based operations and its unwavering commitment to teamwork. The prospect of operating minisubs or diving with noiseless, bubble-free rebreathers thrilled me. Furthermore, their team-centric approach to missions seemed like a natural progression from my rowing experience. Having dedicated eight years to synchronizing eight individuals to row as one and achieve maximum speed, the SEALs represented the next level of teamwork for me. My passion for water and working as part of a team was undeniable. However, it wasn't until LCDR Tough Guy framed it in a relatable context that I connected a purpose to trying out for the SEAL Team.

I faced my fair share of bullying while growing up. I was larger than most children my age—as a first grader, I was as tall as the fourth graders. Compounding the issue, my mother and grandmother insisted that I keep my curly, blond hair long. I didn't mind, as I disliked sitting still for haircuts. However, unbeknownst to me, my hairstyle bore a striking resemblance to that of child actress Shirley Temple. A couple of fourth-grade bullies made the connection, and the nickname stuck, eventually escalating to challenges of whether "Shirley" Mills fought like a girl. Recess often involved impromptu wrestling matches against kids who were faster and stronger than me. I would sprint home after school, navigating the backwoods and creating my own trails to evade the bullies. Over time, as I gained strength and confidence, the bullying subsided, but only after I stood up to them. I learned early on that bullies responded to one thing: being confronted. So when LCDR Tough Guy asked me about my experience with bullying, it resonated deeply, evoking a torrent of memories and emotions, and ultimately connecting me with a purpose for joining the SEAL Team.

Passion is essential, but without purpose, your passion may not be enough to carry you through challenging times. Passions can resemble hobbies—enjoyable activities but not necessarily full-time endeavors. For a hobby to transition into a meaningful career or other serious commitment, you need to discover the purpose in your work. Purpose propels you forward when facing obstacles. It enables you to dig deeper, connecting you with a profound sense of why you should endure pain from sustained effort, frustration from failure, and fear of the unknown. Purpose pushes you beyond perceived limitations and keeps you going when others decide "this isn't fun anymore."

When Instructor Half Butt said, "Y'all been focusing on being a SEAL on a sunny day," he was alluding to the passion one might have for becoming a SEAL but not the underlying purpose of their actions. The same is true for entrepreneurs. It's easy to be passionate about setting your own hours, creating popular products, and perhaps achieving fame and fortune. However, these passion-based thoughts won't sustain you when faced with bankruptcy, rejection, or criticism. Finding purpose in your passion or cultivating passion for your purpose is a crucial component in developing an Unstoppable Mindset.

EXERCISE | **Linking Passion with Purpose**

I do not care if passion or purpose comes first, but you do need both to overcome obstacles on your path to achieving your dreams. When you have decided on a dream worth pursuing, I want you to write down five reasons why it is worth your time and energy. Specifically, think of the reasons from these perspectives:

How does pursuing this dream impact the people I love? It's the pursuit of the dream that I want you to find real purpose in. It is easy to think about the positive outcomes of making this dream your reality, but the hardest part is staying committed to and positive toward the day-to-day work required to make the dream your new reality. For example, in SEAL Team, over 90 percent of our time was spent training for missions that never happened (today's statistics are different). Finding purpose in the day-to-day work is critical to your success.

How does achieving this dream *impact me and those people I love?* The entire point of any exercise in this book is to help you take action toward your dream. Many times, you will find motivation from those you love the most as a source of fuel when you feel like giving up. Use the same envisioning tools from chapter one to help you experience the emotions that will come from achieving your dream, especially as it pertains to those people you care most about who are positively impacted by your success.

Good news! The first step in mindsetting is keeping the Whiner and all its voices in check by being aware of them. Understand that the Whiner is *very* adept at trying to convince us to stay put. It doesn't want you to expend more energy than is absolutely necessary for your own survival. The Whiner will lull you into taking it easy and staying in the comfort zone, while the Winner will press you to try the unknown—to push you to do more. This mental conversation is a daily struggle, which is why I call it mindsetting. It requires you to actively manage this conversation. Sometimes we will conquer the Whiner easily; other days it will be a battle for us, a struggle just to take one action toward our goal. And that is okay. Don't worry. The struggle is normal. It comes with the territory of pursuing something you have never done before. Accept the struggle for what it is—an opportunity to build your strength.

In the next chapter, I am going to share with you how to strengthen the Winner voice and how to use a series of tools and techniques to fuel you through the struggle.

4 Perpetual Fuel

He stood about five foot five inches, but he acted like he was seven feet tall. His back had been broken from a parachute accident, one of many injuries he had sustained over his eighteen years as a SEAL. The right side of his face seemed locked in a smile, while his left side would offer up his emotions at the moment—most of the time something between a growl and a grimace. We called him "Popeye," although not to his face. He was a chief petty officer and the only way we ever addressed him was "Chief." We nicknamed him Popeye because his forearms were abnormally large, and his version of spinach was a sixty-four-ounce 7-Eleven Big Gulp of black coffee and a can of Copenhagen tobacco. He always looked at you with his head cocked to the left, as if he were sizing you up for a fist fight. What he lacked in height, he more than made up for in attitude. One of his favorite expressions was, "Ain't the size of the dog in the fight—it's the size of fight in the dog!"

His other favorite expression was the one he spent the most time proving to us by way of making us work out until we vomited, or sit in cold water until hypothermia set in and then sit there some more. His was like a personal-mindset-training coach, and he would remind us daily of it: "The body obeys the brain," and "The body is a brain-housing group." He would spend hours getting us to our breaking point, where the pain or cold was so intense that we would question our ability to continue. At that point, Instructor Popeye would smile as he said, "Excellent; now we train!" To him, the initial long runs, excessive PT, or cold-water immersions were nothing more than a warm-up. The real training began when we reached a limit in our heads. He wanted us to get comfortable being uncomfortable—*really uncomfortable*. More specifically, he wanted us to be familiar with pushing beyond our preconceived limitations. As soon as we would break through one limit, he would look for us to break the next one. It was a never-ending cycle for him; as far as I could tell, it was how he approached life, and he made it his mission to teach us how to embrace his mindset.

Instructor Popeye was not part of standard SEAL training; he ran a remedial phase called "Rollback Land." The moniker denotes what happens to a BUD/S candidate when they are injured after Hell Week. (If you are injured before Hell Week, a candidate gets "rolled back" to the starting point of first phase.) Anyone spending time with Popeye means they were injured but not badly enough to be medically dropped from the program. In my case, I had made it halfway through second phase (about 3.5 weeks, which is about 5.5 weeks past Hell Week) before my lungs started bleeding. I was pulled out of my original class (Class 181) and put into "Rollback Land" with Instructor Popeye for 5.5 weeks. (I then reentered training just after Hell Week and had to repeat the five-plus weeks of SEAL training.)

Many of us in Rollback Land did not have the best attitudes, including me. The idea that we had to endure more than five weeks of Instructor Popeye and then repeat five weeks of BUD/S training would make any normal person upset, if not downright depressed. I was starting to fall into the latter category. I would go to bed thinking about the negative hypotheticals of "this-sucks-right-now-and-it's-only-going-to-get-worse-when-I-go-back-through-five-weeks-of-misery-all-over-again." I would replay particularly unpleasant training exercises that I knew I would have to repeat such as extended dune runs (I hated running), the training runs for the fourteen-mile timed run, 3.5-mile timed swim, the early morning log PT, surf torture—the list went on. Every time I thought of an evolution I had already performed, I seemed to focus on the pain of having to repeat it again.

I could feel my attitude slipping, and Instructor Popeye saw it too. At first my negativity presented itself in the form of snide remarks to Popeye's overly positive attitude when challenging us by barking out, "Whoever pukes first wins!" (Side note: Mike Ryan typically always won that competition. He was a PT machine, and he's now my brother-in-law. I married his sister—now that's a swim buddy!) I would respond with something sarcastic like, "Oh, can't wait not to win that one." Most of the time, I said it under my breath just out of Popeye's earshot. I kept getting bolder with my comments and getting chuckles from other members of Rollback Land, until one day I said it too loudly.

I regretted it the moment the sarcastic tone of my comment, "Can't wait for more PT," left my mouth. Popeye stopped and spun around like a gorilla ready to attack its foe. He zeroed in on me, staring directly into my eyes. He didn't blink as he said, "Boys, you carry on with the PT. Mr. Mills and I are going over the berm." The berm is a large, Navy-made sand dune created in the late fall to shield the compound from the rougher winter season waves. Its secondary function is to act as a wall from the public and, in this case, my Rollback Land classmates. I was about to get one-on-one training with Chief Popeye, and I was not looking forward to it.

"Ensign Mills, I noticed your attitude decline the moment you joined my training program, and it's time we have a 'conversation'"—he raised both index fingers and used them as quotation marks as he said the word *conversation*—"about attitude."

I tried for a moment to brush off my comment to see if it would lessen my ensuing punishment, with a half-hearted, "Ahh, Chief, you know I was just kidding."

He looked at me with his head cocked to the left and said, "No, you are not, and I am not either. Hit surf, Ensign Mills. Time to do your laundry and wash that bad attitude out of you."

I spent the entire PT session doing "my laundry" while he gave me attitude-adjustment training. The drill was tedious and freezing. It comprised wading out to chest-deep water, taking off one piece of clothing, such as my "blouse" (an old World War II–styled green shirt), and vigorously pretending to wash it in the surf until he decided I'd washed it enough, at which point he would yell, "Dry!" No walking was allowed. I would run the seventy-five yards back to him, place the shirt neatly on the dry sand above the high-water mark, roll it in sand until completely covered, then run back into the surf zone to "wash" the next article of clothing. By the end of the drill, I was completely naked (the public is not allowed on this portion of beach) and my clothes were laid out on the beach like a series of Legos all in position ready to be connected to form a fully uniformed BUD/S candidate.

Once all my laundry was in the "dry cycle," as he put it, he had me lie flat in only about six to nine inches of water with my head toward the sea. I couldn't see the swells coming and had to time my breaths as the waves washed over me twice: once as they rolled to shore and a second time as they receded back to sea. He called this the "spin cycle," and it was in this cycle that he added his own form of detergent: his mindset philosophy. The process ended by putting one piece of clothing on at a time as I went back out to chest-deep water. The idea was that when I put those clothes back on I had "washed" the bad attitude out of me. Of course, he did not stop there, because, well, laundry isn't complete until it goes through a dryer cycle. His "dryer cycle" involved dune sprints and, for good measure, eight-count body builders (a push-up with squat thrust and jump), and lunges between sprints up the thirty-yard sand dune.

I puked—several times.

His mindset detergent was powerful. My choice was to endure, or quit. He was known for getting candidates to ring the bell, and this was definitely the kind of drill that would get one seriously thinking about dropping out. As miserable as I was, and I was very miserable, I heard what he was saying, and I knew he was right. My attitude needed an adjustment. I was having my own form of a pity party, and that negative attitude was infecting the whole Rollback class. I have always remembered his words of mindset wisdom and, over the years, honed them to help course correct not only myself but also friends (who ask), teammates, coworkers, my four boys, and, of course, my clients. Except we don't do our "laundry" in cold water. We go to the "gym." I call this gym the Positivity Gym, and every one of us has this gym. We just have to learn how to use the equipment.

POSITIVITY GYM BASIC TRAINING

Have you ever conducted a genetic test, such as 23andMe, where they take a sample of your DNA and give you a report about your genetic makeup? Perhaps you have. Let me ask you: Were you one of the lucky ones that got the positivity gene? Grab your report and scroll down. It comes right after the leadership gene, and just before your success gene. Did you screen positive for it?

Wait, what? You can't find it, nor can you find the leadership and success genes?

Well, guess what. That's because there is no such thing as a positivity gene—it doesn't exist, just like there is no such thing as a leadership or success gene. Yep, that's right, your attitude is yours and yours alone. That's rule number one. You have to train yourself to be positive.

Rule 1—You Own Your Attitude

There are very, *very* few things in life we can control, but those few can determine our direction. Your attitude is one of the single most important things you can control, and if you are not careful, you will let others influence and sometimes even control your attitude for you. The reason attitude is so critical to your success is that it directly influences how you communicate, collaborate, and contribute. People experience you through your attitude. Your attitude drives your action and how people act toward you.

You might be asking, "If attitude is so important, why didn't you list it as one of the three pillars in the Mindset Loop of thoughts, focus, and beliefs?" That's a good question, so let's go.

Attitude comes from thoughts and feelings. When we attach to a thought and focus on it, we generate a feeling. Thoughts and feelings work hand in hand. The more you focus on them, the more they feed off each other to produce an emotion. Psychologists call this interaction the *thought-feeling loop*. This loop creates energy, which is called an emotion.

I love how emotion is described in the book *The 15 Commitments of Conscious Leadership* by Jim Dethmer, Diana Chapman, and Kaley Klemp. They refer to emotion as "E-Motion" or Energy in Motion. Emotions can be momentary (such as expressing *how* you feel when you feel it) or they can stick around, swirling inside you and sometimes causing all kinds of problems by stressing you out. The key takeaway here is to remember that thoughts and feelings generate emotions, and these emotions set your attitude. And who controls which thoughts you connect with? *You!* Hence, your attitude is up to you. At the right is how I visualize the thought-feeling loop.

You have no one to blame but yourself on the attitude you *decide* to embrace. If Viktor Frankl could find a positive attitude while imprisoned at Auschwitz, surely you can learn to decide your own attitude!

Rule 2—The Body and Brain Are Swim Buddies

One of the single most important lessons learned during SEAL training is the body-brain connection. Whether it was Instructors Half Butt, Psycho, Popeye, Aloha, Antichrist, Nutball, Boston, or any of the other colorful personalities in training, they all adhered to the importance of this body-brain connection. Of course, they didn't call it the body-brain connection. They referred to it as our single most important "weapons platform."[1] They routinely reminded us that we were no use to the SEAL Teams, the Navy, or even our country if we did not learn to harness the power of our weapons platform. They would reason, "What good does it do us to give you expensive equipment to use if you cannot even control the body that is using

[1] A weapons platform can be a boat, helicopter, truck, or some other type of vehicle or structure on which to mount or attach weapons. SEAL instructors use the term to describe the human body as a weapons platform in the sense that our weapons depend upon our body that is carrying them.

it?" BUD/S and all the post-training classes after graduation centered around the control of the most important weapon on the battlefield: our bodies and how we use them.

I can still hear Instructor Boston in his south Boston accent through his ever-present electronic megaphone, repeating, "Yah body obeys yah brain. If it's thah othah way around, yah ain't making it through." Instructor Popeye would chirp constantly about our bodies being a "brain-housing group." He loved delivering scientific dissertations on how all the systems of the body are designed to support the brain while we were treading water keeping our elbows above our heads and wearing diving weight belts. Instructor Antichrist never said much besides his grunts, but when he did string a sentence or two together, he instructed us to "make your body obey your brain's commands—command now or quit and save me the time." When Instructor Aloha (a big-wave surfer from the North Shore of Oahu) conducted "remedial breath-holding classes," he reminded us that "your body is trying to take charge; don't let it—put it in its place and continue mission" (in this case, the mission was staying relaxed and continuing to hold our breath).

All teams in SEAL Team are based on the swim-buddy construct. Two swim pairs make up a fire team, two fire teams form a squad, and two squads are a platoon. (As the Army and Navy work closer together today, SEAL Team has adopted an Army term, "squadron," which is little larger than two SEAL platoons.) Popeye referred to our vital weapons system as swim buddies. The way Popeye saw it, the brain and body were swim buddies; they needed each other to survive, thrive, and, of course, conduct missions. However, swim pairs need one person to take the lead. Whether you are walking through the jungle, busting through a door, or conducting combat swimmer missions, there is always one of the pair taking the lead.

Of course, in SEAL Team, that position rotates depending on the mission. In the case of our individual "weapons system," that leader is the brain. Popeye often reminded us that the body would try to assume the leadership position when it was pushed outside its comfort zone. He would constantly tell us that it was in his job description to push our bodies outside their comfort zones so he could teach our brains how to lead our bodies during these times of discomfort.

Popeye was quite good at his job.

What does the body-brain connection mean to you? Your body fuels your brain, and the better fueled your brain is, the better it will operate, so it can in turn take better care of your body. The better each swim buddy functions, the more powerful and potent they can be as a team. In other words, they will be better at making the hard decisions to keep pressing on when things get tough. By the way, things always get tough when you are in pursuit of something you have never done before. There have been hundreds of books written about each of the three components I am about to list when it comes to the basic building blocks of your weapons platform. This book is not about educating you on every detail of sleep, nutrition, and exercise, but it is about ensuring you understand these levers and how critical they are to your performance. I refer to these building blocks with my coaching and speaking clients in the form of a question that I ask routinely: "How well did you SEE this week?" Like most actions I coach, I organize them into acronyms so others (and I!) can remember them. SEE stands for sleep, eat, and exercise, and they are in that order for a reason. Sleep is number one, eating is number two, and exercise rounds out the bottom of the priority list when it comes to ensuring your body-brain swim pair is in good functioning order.

Sleep

I had a rowing coach who used to say, "You'll get all the sleep you want when you're dead." My teammates and I even fell for it a few times, but the truth is, if you want to perform, you *must* get good and sufficient amounts of sleep. Here are a few of the basics to consider to ensure that you do get quality sleep:

- **Physical space:** Make sure that the room is dark (so dark you can't see your hand six inches in front of your face), cool (less than sixty-five degrees), and quiet or with some kind of white noise (there are plenty of sleep sound machines for sale). A weighted blanket is a plus; I use one and find it helpful. The right mattress is also critical. If you're thinking, *Ah, I don't need to spend too much on a high-quality mattress*, remind yourself that about one-third of your life is spent on it.
- **Nutrition:** Be aware that alcohol crushes your REM sleep (that's the deep sleep you need to restore and recharge). If you need to be at your best the next day, go without alcohol the night before. Experts recommend no caffeine after 2:00 p.m. I follow that rule; it works well for me. Reduce your water intake a couple hours before bedtime; getting up to pee in the middle of night breaks up your sleep and creates opportunities for your mind to reactivate and think of things that will keep you awake.
- **Exercise:** Experts suggest getting some sunlight throughout your day, as it helps with melatonin production (your go-to-sleep chemical), so kill two birds with one stone and conduct a workout outside (walking counts). There are numerous studies to support the link between exercising and good sleep.

Research it for yourself, but some amount of daily exercise (again, walking counts) will aid in a good night's slumber.

I am admittedly only scratching the surface here, and if you want to go deep on sleep, here are two books I really enjoy: *Why We Sleep* by Matthew Walker and *Sleep for Success* by Dr. James B. Mass. Doing the above will get you well on your way to great, consistent sleep, and your swim buddies will thank you for it—I promise!

Eat

I am not a nutritionist, but I was a certified optimal performance trainer for over a dozen years while running Perfect Fitness, and I learned the basics of nutrition. I am not going to tell you what to eat, but I am going to share with you three critical rules that my nutritionist shares with me (yes, I use a nutritionist, and he's invaluable to helping me perform at my best). His name is Jon Andersen (founder of Deep Water Method), and his rules are simple and very effective:

1. Never be hungry.
2. Eat on a schedule.
3. Eat something even when you don't feel hungry on your schedule.

Jon is a performance nutritionist, and his focus is helping people perform better. He compares our metabolism to a fire that needs to be constantly stoked. However, it must be fed the proper kinds of wood. If you use plastic (man-made foods), it might burn, yet it will give off all kinds of toxins. Use whole foods and eat every three hours between five and six times a day while following his three rules, and you *will* notice your energy improving within forty-eight hours. (Of course, there are different meal plans for different types of results: gaining muscle, losing weight, or managing weight.) My focus is ensuring you have the energy required to keep taking daily action; consult a nutritionist if you want more out of your meal plan than just energy.

However, I completely understand that you might not be a fan of what I like or have different nutrition goals than I do, and I totally get it. What I am trying to drive home for you is to have a plan to get the most out of what you put in your body. There are plenty of nutrition plans out there—find the one that works for you. The point is to eat like an athlete, because you are one—an athlete taking daily action!

Exercise

With my team, I invented the Perfect Pushup (along with about a hundred other fitness products). I climb mountains to stay in shape (including three of the Seven Summits). I have trained for over seven years—six days a week as a SEAL—and rowed competitively for nine years. I have done *a lot* of physical exercise in my life. Yet here I am listing it as the third priority on our weapons platform performance-requirements list. That's because most things in life are a part of a system; they interoperate in some form or fashion and depend on each other to perform better. Get little sleep for days and eat junk and guess how motivated you will be to exercise. Not much. In fact, the only motivation you will have is to seek the next quick fix to feel a little bit better.

Quick fixes come in many forms, from sugary foods and highly caffeinated drinks to alcohol and drugs. Allow this cycle of highs and lows to continue and you will find yourself overweight, out of shape, exhausted, and completely unmotivated to do anything but focus on simply getting by. I have been there myself. In the Michael Myers comedy movie series Austin Powers, Myers plays several characters, one of whom is called Fat Bastard. This wildly obese Scot, at one point in the series, explains why he is the way he is by stating in a heavy Scottish accent: "I'm unhappy because I'm fat, and I'm fat because I'm unhappy." I call this loop the Fat Bastard syndrome, and I use it as a metaphor to express how an unhealthy habit creates an unhappy emotion and how they feed on each other.

I am using this expression as an example of how sleep, eating, and exercise are all linked together. If one is off, the other two will be negatively impacted. In this case, I want you to realize that the better sleep and nutrition you have, the more energy you have to exercise. When you exercise, your body creates healthy, feel-good chemicals, such as serotonin and dopamine, that make you feel somewhere between good and great. When you feel good, you will want to continue feeling good, so you will exercise again. In this case, the Fat Bastard syndrome works in the opposite way too: "I'm happy because I exercise, and I exercise because I'm happy." When the first two are in alignment, you will actually look forward to working out. I know it might sound crazy to some, but if you feel good, exercise will only help you feel better (there are of course outliers of this—too much exercise can be a bad thing, so always check with your doctor and get your body systems checked before embarking on any exercise plan).

Before you start to dismiss exercise as a nice-to-have and not a must-have in your weekly routine, let me remind you that you are an athlete regardless of your profession. Our bodies are designed to perform at their best when we care for them through sleep, nutrition, and exercise. Now you may think I am overdoing it with calling us all "athletes," but I am not, and here is an example to prove it. I am on the professional speaking circuit—I give about fifty speeches a year to audiences as large as forty thousand people. I customize my speeches, so there is more prep and practice that goes into my speaking, but I know my information cold.

I once wore a heart rate monitor for a *Be Unstoppable* speech. (I give several types of speeches, but my focus is helping people *be unstoppable* at leading themselves and their teams.) This particular day I was speaking to a small group of approximately sixty senior executives. I knew no one in the audience, but I knew what I was talking about. I put the monitor on fifteen minutes before the speech, spoke for an hour, and took it off fifteen minutes afterward. I burned 976 calories; my heart rate spiked to 85 percent of my max and averaged 71 percent over the duration of the speech. And a reminder, I was presenting information I knew; I did not have a huge risk of failure, nor was I dependent on this speech for a sales quota or a fundraising goal.

Imagine what my heart rate would be if there was more on the line for me financially or professionally. My point is, no matter what type of work you are in, your body will be dealing with stress, and how well it handles stress is directly correlated to . . . can you guess?

How well you SEE (sleep, eat, and exercise)!

Last point before I offer up some simple exercise guidelines. Going after a dream is work. John C. Maxwell says it best: "Dreams only work if you do." It's an old but accurate expression. Work as defined mathematically looks like this:

$$W = (M \times A) \times D$$

W = (Mass multiplied by Acceleration) multiplied by Distance. In physics terms, energy must be expended to perform work, and there are plenty of mathematical equations to define and quantify work. I am not asking you to quantify your ability to work, but I am imploring you to understand the direct correlation between your ability to perform work and your ability to accomplish your dream.

Exercise builds strength and endurance that you will need in boatloads depending on the size of your dream. Please, *please* think of exercise as a mission critical daily action that will help you build the stamina required to achieve your dream—whatever your dream, including "nonathletic" events such as writing a book, or creating art, or giving a speech, or leading a business team. It does *not* matter what your dream is. You will need endurance to persist, and that comes from exercise.

When I use the term *exercise,* I am referring to some kind of "sustained physical effort." I am not suggesting you need to be an Ironman triathlete or a Navy SEAL or perform some kind of superhuman level of effort for hours and hours each day. On the contrary, I want you to find some physical effort that you enjoy and incorporate it into your weekly and daily schedule. Here are a few simple rules to understand about exercise, listed in order of importance:

1. **Frequency**—exercise is an accumulative process. You can work out in five-minute increments every hour on the hour for eight hours, and that will count as a total of forty minutes of exercise for that day. If you are just starting out and have never really exercised, focus on frequency first. I would much prefer you do ten minutes a day every day than seventy minutes once a week. Building the habit is the most important first step. Please think of exercise as an event in your calendar; it is a daily action item that you can execute on. Incidentally, when calendaring exercise, consider this: the most popular times are in the morning, during lunch, or after work. Again, make it work for you, but find a time every day for exercise, and I promise you will be happy you did it.
2. **Duration**—once you have an exercise frequency and are comfortable with it (dare I say, even enjoying it?), then you can look to add time to your exercising. Depending on your

goals, duration is an important metric of exercise. Over time, our body-brain swim buddies are very adept at figuring out ways to reduce our energy output during a repeat exercise routine. For example, let's say you have decided to walk one mile a day on a treadmill at three miles per hour. The first day you walk, you burn two hundred calories. A few weeks later, you will have only burned perhaps 175 calories. A couple of things are happening. One, you are getting in better shape, so your body doesn't need as many calories to walk the same distance, and two, your brain is working behind the scenes with your body to optimize your stride and breathing more efficiently every time you take a step. This is why you will have gains early from exercise routines that then plateau unless you adjust duration along with the next two rules: intensity and type.

3. **Intensity**—this is about how hard you are exercising, and it's measured through heart rate. Once you have frequency and duration dialed in, use intensity to improve your exercise gains (*if* this is something you seek). Knowing your max heart rate (HR) is important, and here is a simple way to do it: 220 minus your age = your max HR. Multiply your max HR by .55, .65, and .85 respectively to determine your HR training zones. This is a very simplistic way to get started, and I highly recommend researching HR training zones for your specific exercise routines. Better yet, hire a personal trainer to help you get started or improve your exercise routines. The .55, .65, and .85 represent 55 percent, 65 percent, and 85 percent of your max HR. These zones will help you modulate your training to improve your conditioning and also give you targets to focus on while exercising. The first two zones, 55

and 65 percent, are considered fat-burning zones while the zones above that are typically shorter in duration and are for more intense cardiovascular conditioning. (You do improve your aerobic conditioning in lower HR zones as well, so do not think you have to go hard to get the benefits—*not true*!)

4. **Type**—as mentioned earlier, our brain-body swim pair is adept at making us more energy efficient every time we perform the same movement pattern. Furthermore, expect to get bored doing the same exercise over and over again, which is why it is really important, not just physically but mentally and emotionally, to rotate among different forms of exercise. Walking, swimming, biking, hiking, running, rowing, and at least fifty other forms of exercise are out there. Try some that you have never done before; you just might like it, or perhaps you might like that challenge of mastering a new form. The point is that variety is the spice of life, and that definitely applies to exercise too! Rotating from walking one day to a stationary bike the next will not only help your body get more gains but also give you something to look forward to.

There are of course more variables you can adjust over time with exercise, but the four listed above will get you into the winner's column for most any dream you seek to achieve. If your dream requires more, please consult a professional trainer to help you avoid muscle imbalances and improve speed, agility, or elasticity (to name a few). And if you are like me and are great at making excuses for why you cannot exercise, then here's one exercise routine you can do anywhere, anytime: the body builder exercise. The basic concept is to do a push-up but you have to stand up in between each push-up. Like all exercises, it can be made more intense with just a few simple modifications.

The Body Builder Exercise for Beginners

1. Start with feet shoulder width apart. Squat down while placing your hands on the ground.
2. Extend one leg at a time until you are in the plank position (i.e., the top position of the push-up).
3. Perform a push-up (place hands one hand width wider than your shoulders).
4. Bring one leg at a time up to your chest to return to the squat position.
5. Stand up and count out loud to yourself.

The Body Builder Exercise for Intermediates

1. Perform the same as above except instead of extending one leg at a time, jump both legs out together. This will require you to use more core muscles (abs, lower back).
2. Repeat the same before standing up: pull both legs in together after conducting the push-up.

The Body Builder Exercise for Experts

1. The same as above except when you complete the exercise, instead of standing, jump as high as you can.

2. Make it even more intense by incorporating a pull-up bar into your jump. As you jump, grab the bar (even a strong tree branch will do), perform a pull-up, and then return to the starting position.

If you stick out your tongue and contort your face into an odd expression while doing the above, you are essentially activating nearly all six hundred muscles in the body! And, yes, that includes your heart muscle. This is a highly intense aerobic exercise. I strongly recommend you take it slow (after you have spoken to your doctor, of course). You now have an exercise that will shut down the Whiner.

Rule 3—There Is Always *a Positive to a Negative*

Nature is built on balance, called "homeostasis." For some, the experience of a negative event is considered just that—a negative outcome they wished hadn't happened. But for others, the negative event can actually be a positive event. I know—you are already challenging this statement by thinking of catastrophic events such as a hurricane, tornado, earthquake, tsunami, and the myriad natural disasters, to say nothing of the massive number of tragic human events of loss and suffering around the world. Every event is of course different and distinct, and I am certainly not trying to minimize any event of human suffering or loss. But what I want you to understand is that the laws of nature—seeking balance—apply to all of us, meaning there is always an equal and opposite reaction to every event—good or bad.

From the science of quantum mechanics to the ancient Eastern philosophies, there is a balance to everything. For every negative, there is an equal and opposite positive. Like yin and yang, negative and positive coexist in equilibrium. I am not a physicist—I scraped by both physics classes at the Naval Academy—but it's very important for you to realize that you cannot have a negative without a positive and vice versa.

Why is this important to becoming unstoppable in achieving your goals?

Because you will face all kinds of obstacles along your journey, and your ability to overcome these obstacles will define your direction and destiny. As thought leaders from John Adams to Deepak Chopra have said many times: "Obstacles are nothing more than opportunities in disguise." When you accept that there is always a positive to a negative, then there is no such thing as an obstacle. It is just another opportunity for you to learn something new. This is easily written but hard to embrace, especially when those around you are convinced the obstacle is too great to overcome. There are so many people willing to quickly tell you what you can or cannot do, based on their own beliefs of what they can or can't do. Do not allow other people to set your limitations for you. Adopting Rule 3 requires practice, which is exactly what we are going to do next. When you combine these three rules, you will find you have all the components you need to persevere confidently in the direction of your dream.

We head for the Positivity Gym because building a positive attitude is a muscle, and muscles are built in gyms. Positivity requires practice, and you can practice in the "gym" anytime and anywhere. Imagine for a moment you are on a deserted island, and the only way to escape is to swim, but you aren't strong enough to swim the distance required to a much bigger, lusher island that you can see in the distance, just on the edge of the horizon. To get our bodies in shape, we need to perform some exercises. We don't need many exercises, but we need just the right ones that will help our minds and bodies escape this desolate island for a bigger, better island within our grasp.

This simple metaphor captures the challenge of pursuing something new. Your current location may be so familiar that it's like an island, which over time becomes more desolate as you become more familiar with it. But the tide is rising (or perhaps more apropos, the sea level is rising) and your island of familiarity is feeling smaller and smaller. You decide you are fed up living on this shrinking island and want to get to the new, lush, beautiful island you see in the distance. But you are scared—scared of getting eaten by sharks or drowning or being swept away. To overcome your fears and fire yourself up, hit the Positivity Gym on your island.

Exercise 1—Stretch—stretching your mind past the fear of your negative thoughts and opening yourself up to the possibility of positive outcomes. It is totally normal to be scared of the unknown. We are conditioned to place more emphasis on negative thoughts than positive thoughts. Typically, we tend to overemphasize the negative of the unknown (e.g., "there are sharks that will eat me"), which can fill us with dread and prevent us from taking action toward our goal and keep us stuck where we are at. The key concept behind "stretching" is to make the fear of staying put *greater* than the fear of going forward. This requires you to stretch your thoughts into the future and see yourself staying put on an island that is slowly shrinking. What happens if you stay on that island for one year? Three years? Would you rather drown not taking action? Until we make the fear of staying put greater than the fear of trying something new, we will find reasons to stay put. This exercise is about making the fear of staying put greater than the fear of moving forward. When you have successfully envisioned this, then your stretching exercise is complete—move to exercise 2!

Exercise 2—Push/Pull—all weight-lifting workouts require equal and opposite muscle group routines. If you do not do this, you will build muscle imbalances. Perform a push exercise followed by a pull exercise. Push away the negative thought, and the moment after you push it away, pull in the positive helpful thought that will assist you in accomplishing your goal (i.e., swimming to the new destination). At first, this might seem hard, because negative thoughts are so easy to focus on. As you pull in more positive thoughts ("there has to be a way I can get to the new island" or "I know I can figure it out"), keep your focus on those thoughts that will help you achieve your goal. Each time you perform this exercise, ask yourself, *Is this thought helpful or hurtful for my progress toward my goal?* Make this a habit and then proceed to the next exercise, the dead lift.

Exercise 3—Dead Lift—one of the most important total-body strength-building exercises there is, this exercise requires you to dig deep and lift heavy weight. Do this properly and you will strengthen all the major muscle groups of your body. The metaphorical exercise for your mind is to dig deep on curiosity. Get insanely curious about how you can overcome the obstacles your Whiner has been whining about. Curiosity leads to creativity, which leads to gaining confidence on how to come up with solutions to perceived obstacles. For instance, *Do I have to swim the entire way? Is there a current that will push me? When are sharks least hungry? Can I figure out a way to harness the wind and waves?*

As you dig deep into asking yourself these questions, you discover new ways to look at making the crossing. You realize you don't have to swim. You can cut down a tree, make a surfboard out of it, build a sail from the palm fronds, and conduct your journey in the middle of the day when the wind, waves, and currents are in your favor and the sharks are not hungry! Now you're getting excited and confident about your new goal and are ready for exercise 4.

Exercise 4—Core—core exercises are an essential part of every exercise routine; they connect your upper and lower body to ensure you can perform multi-joint movements. For the mindset, your core exercises are positive affirmations or mantras that act as *can-do* reminders. When making an affirmation, stay in the present: "I am a strong swimmer." "I am a great problem solver." "I keep going no matter what happens." Positive affirmations are important because neuroscientists have discovered that one negative comment can require many positive comments just to offset it; if you want to be in the positive can-do winner's column, you need upward of five positive comments to beat back the negativity of your Whiner.

Positive affirmations or mantras help shift your focus and energy into a helpful state of mind. As you shape your board and practice your moves with your new sail, you start to fail. You get frustrated, and as you do, you remind yourself again and again and again that you can do it. You tell yourself, *Even if my sail breaks, I can still paddle on my board, and even if my board breaks, I can use half of it as a kick-board to get there.* You remind yourself of your other exercises, which leads you to create a circuit routine with your four exercises. You finish with your core exercises, take a break, and repeat your exercise routine again.

LEAVING YOUR SHRINKING ISLAND

Spend the time in the Positivity Gym and, before you know it, you aren't fearing your journey to the new island—you are looking forward to it. The night before you are to leave, you can barely sleep. You have performed your Positivity Gym routines so many times that you have already envisioned what you are going to do when you reach that new island. The morning comes, and it's time to go. You conduct your Positivity Gym routine again. Stretch—you know why you're leaving, and you don't fear the path ahead; Push/Pull—negative thoughts are pushed aside and your mind is pulling in positive can-do thoughts for each leg of your journey; Dead Lift—you're curious about how your new board and sail will work, you're curious about the sea state (wind, currents, and waves) that can help propel you even faster to your destination; and Core—you remind yourself of all the work you have done, you even compliment yourself on getting to this point, you marvel at your handiwork of your board/sail innovation, and then you give yourself the final core exercise: "Let's go—I got this!"

The trip has all kinds of challenges. The sail sometimes pushes you backward. You fall off your board multiple times. You think you see a shark following below you (then you realize it's your sail's shadow!). The wind changes, which then changes the course of the waves. You adapt by using your Positivity Gym exercises. You learn to tack with your sail system and again start making progress. The island is in plain sight now. Your confidence swells. You tell yourself, *You are doing it. You got this!* You fall off your board, but this time you laugh because you realize you can touch the sandy bottom and decide to walk for a while, enjoying the final leg of your journey.

By the time you arrive, you are smiling and telling yourself, *I can't believe I worried about this journey for so long. That was actually fun. I wonder where I can go next.* Along the way, you make mental notes on how to modify your sail craft to make it faster and more maneuverable. Your mind is already back in the Positivity Gym, thinking about how to improve your ideas for the yet-to-be-determined next journey. You arrive. You are tired, but it's a great tired because you are satisfied with yourself. Your confidence has grown. The sea is no longer a place to be feared. Instead, it becomes a source of inspiration that can help transport you to a new destination. You get a piña colada and sit on a beautiful beach, and as you watch the sunset, you start dreaming up your next goal.

Okay, you may say, "Alden, that's a little bit of a stretch for a metaphor." Sure, your remote island is unrealistic, but that's not the point. I want you to visualize the current shrinking island because that is what life can be like if you decide never to take action toward your goal. You remain stuck on your island of sameness guaranteed by your decision not to move forward. You do not act on your goal or, worse, you give up because the fear of staying where you are is less than the fear of not getting where you want to go.

There are all kinds of forces at work trying to push you back to your island of the known. The wind, water, and waves are actually external forces you will inevitably face from other people: friends, family, experts saying, "You're not ready. You're not enough. It can't be done." You must learn to push them aside and harness them as fuel to propel you forward. Curiosity, and the creativity that comes from it, is your secret weapon, and it is activated by getting deeply curious about how to overcome obstacles. When you learn to coach yourself by speaking positively to yourself, you realize that what you say to yourself matters. Those comments keep you seeking solutions instead of focusing on the fear.

The Positivity Gym works because you must think of it like a gym—a place to exercise, a place to practice techniques that help you get stronger. When you incorporate the exercise routines of the Positivity Gym with the three Rules of Positivity Gym—Rule 1: You own your attitude; Rule 2: Your brain/body are swim buddies; and Rule 3: There's *always* a positive to a negative—then you will discover your greatest challenge in life is your ability to dream up greater dreams!

EXERCISE | **Play the Opposite Game**

Here is a powerful technique for using the fear of an obstacle as fuel: *play the opposite game.* Because nature always seeks balance and we know there is a positive to a negative, when you encounter what appears to be a negative experience, an insurmountable obstacle, or a serious setback, force yourself to come up with three positives to the situation you are experiencing.

I use this technique while coaching executives. It forces them to switch their focus. Typically, I will ask them to take a casual walk in conjunction with thinking creatively. The walk elevates their blood flow while increasing their breathing (sending more oxygen to the brain). Consider a situation from a different perspective that can gain you insights in overcoming the obstacle. Trust me: there is a positive for each negative. It just comes in a different wrapper and it requires you to get creative to find it. But once you find it, you will also discover additional and vital can-do energy to fuel you (and your team) to succeed in the face of fear. Play the opposite game with a friend, colleague, child, or teammate. When something is not going your way, play the opposite game. It could be as simple as not getting a parking spot near the entrance of the store (positive: yes, I get to walk farther and burn extra calories) or an appliance breaks (more time to bond in the kitchen with the family) or a job deadline gets moved up (great, I want to start a new job earlier). Whatever the scenario, force yourself to find at least two positives to the negative you are first experiencing. Write down a recent negative experience here and list two positives to that negative experience.

Negative Experience:

____
____
____
____
____
____
____
____

Positives:

1. ____________________________________

2. ____________________________________

through a whole series of mistakes we'd made and what we could learn from them.

Some of the mistakes the senior SEAL made sure we made, such as walking through the bottom of the small canyon where an enemy could shoot down on us from both flanks. There were lots of tactical discussions, but the most strategic one I learned that day was the importance of staying calm in the face of fear—in this case, an ambush. The moment I let my mind drift to the negative was the moment I lost my ability to think creatively about how to solve the problem I was in quickly and effectively, and that's what this chapter is about—helping you deal with the ambushes life throws at you.

AMYGDALA 101

Training for an ambush is like training for running your ship aground or hitting submerged obstacles—it is something no one wants to happen because you must react to a completely unexpected (and often violent) situation. You may never experience a military ambush or hitting a submerged obstacle with your ship, but I am certain you have been "ambushed" many times.

I use the term *ambush* as a metaphor for the unexpected happening to you. It might occur when someone calls you out for poor performance in front of a room full of colleagues or teammates. It could be a flanking ambush where you were fired because another company bought yours and you're out of a job. Perhaps you get ambushed from the rear, where something happens you did not see coming that stops you in your tracks. Sometimes, these ambushes can feel like they are coming at you from all sides. When an ambush happens, there can be an immediate sense of despair and helplessness—a point when we look inside ourselves and ask, *Why is this happening to me?* When we attach to these selfish and pity-oriented thoughts, we activate this little almond-size element of our brain called the amygdala.

This organ deep inside our brain is our survivability reflex organ. Think of it like a little nitro-booster for a car engine that momentarily revs the engine extra high to produce extra horsepower. When a nitro-booster is released into a car's engine, the highly flammable liquid supercharges the car's engine for a brief period of time. In the case of our bodies, our nitro-booster brain organ (the amygdala) secretes its own form of highly flammable liquids called cortisol and adrenaline. These two hormone superchargers hit our bloodstreams with adrenaline, which elevates our heart rates (revs our engines), while cortisol redirects our digestive systems to find quick-burning fuel from sugar versus fat. They work together to keep feeding our engine (body) to rapidly burn fuel (sugar) to keep our heart rates up so we can move quickly to either fighting or fleeing. In some extreme cases, our bodies can get so overwhelmed by the immediate secretion of these two chemicals that we freeze. I call these reactions the three Fs of an ambush: fight, flight, or freeze.

The amygdala has been widely researched over the past twenty years, and the results have helped researchers understand not only how it works but also, most importantly, how to control it. It's very understandable, when an unexpected event happens to us, to have an amygdala response. For example, the best basketball shooter on your team cannot take the game-winning shot because she is double-teamed, so she passes the ball to you. There is one second left on the game clock, and you must make the shot to win. Or the executive team tells you at the last minute you are the one making the sales pitch that could save the year in sales quotas for your company. Stress is stress, and you do not need to experience the stress of someone shooting at you to experience an ambush.

We all put pressure on ourselves, but when someone or some situation unexpectedly places even more pressure on you, that is a prime time for your amygdala to fire. And when it does, there is one more thing you *must* appreciate: it redirects blood flow from the front of your brain (prefrontal cortex) to the back of your brain. The front of your brain is where creative problem solving (and compassion, which is key in collaboration) occurs. In keeping with my car analogy, it allows you to drive your car like a Formula 1 driver—swerving, weaving, dodging, and drifting. The back of the brain is not nearly that creative. It is much more like a drag strip racer, either burning rubber or going fast in a straight line for a short period of time, when the focus is on much simpler directions: forward, stop, or reverse.

The way to conquer an ambush is by using your innate creativity to overcome the uncertainty of the moment. Yet our brains have this ancient biological reflex of prioritizing surviving over creativity. Still, the large majority of the ambushes we encounter today require creative solutions rather than survival reflexes of fight, flight, or freeze. I share this important neurological fact with you because, anytime you decide to pursue a dream, it will involve taking actions that you haven't performed before, which heightens the likelihood of encountering lots of amygdala ambushes. If you aren't careful, a few amygdala ambushes might cause you to give up on your dream.

To override your amygdala, two really important tips are:

1. **Be aware**—the first best tip is recognizing when you are in an ambush. The moment you recognize that, you will be able to keep your composure and act on tip 2.

2. **Breathe!** In SEAL Team, they now have platoons learn the box breath, a series of three-second breaths and holds starting through the nose and exhaling through the mouth with two breath holds (one as you breathe in and one after you exhale). This series of breaths allows blood flow to continue to the front of your brain to help you think under pressure.

   (Here's how to do the box breath: Breathe in through your nose for three seconds. Hold for three seconds. Exhale for three seconds. Hold for three seconds. Repeat this five times. For more on breathing techniques and learning how to hijack the amygdala, check out James Nestor's book *Breath*.)

It may seem odd that the first tip is to just recognize the ambush, but the more you get accustomed to recognizing situations that are potential amygdala alerts, the more you'll be intentional about doing something about it versus doing an amygdala knee-jerk-style reaction of fight, flight, or freeze. In SEAL Team, you train to recognize potential lethal-ambush situations so you can avoid them. After all, the best way to handle an ambush is to not put yourself in the position to get ambushed. Of course, that is not possible all of the time, especially when you are entering unfamiliar territory, such as going after a goal you have never pursued before.

Back to the car analogy: When you learn to drive, what's the number one skill the instructor wants you to learn? The skill of learning to drive defensively, to always be on the lookout for that potential ambush by other drivers either not seeing you or not paying attention to the road. I'm not suggesting you go through life on the defensive, but when it comes to trying new things, practice anticipating potential ambushes. The act of preparation can help you remain calm and creative when and if something unexpected occurs, which will reduce the chances of the amygdala hijacking your responses.

INTERNAL AMBUSHES

Up until now, the ambushes I've touched on have been external ones—those that happen to you and against which you must defend yourself through calm, creative thinking. However, some of the most challenging ambushes are the ones we stage against ourselves. How do we ambush ourselves?

By becoming attached to our thoughts.

If we aren't careful, we will allow a series of thoughts, which I call a narrative or negative script, to run on repeat in our heads enough times that they will trigger amygdala-like responses. You know those moments before you are about to give a speech and your mouth goes dry, hands get sweaty, beads of perspiration form on your forehead and under your armpits, and you start getting the shakes? Or the times just before we take the test on which we need to get a certain grade to pass the class? Or maybe it's the tryout for the team we so desperately want to make or the sales pitch we must land to hit the quota?

How about the times when you're just dreaming about the idea of trying out for the varsity team or thinking about making that new idea into reality or challenging that person's direction because you think you have a better plan? You know those moments. The ones that you have only thought about privately. The ones that you haven't even shared with anyone yet while you deliberate on whether your idea is any good. These are places where we can get ambushed too, and they are brutal ambushes that can leave no survivors—your confidence or conviction to share or press on with your idea can fall victim to this attack.

How many times have we all had a great idea but decided that it was not worth pursuing because "it wouldn't work" or "it was stupid" or "I can't do it" or "[insert your excuse here]"? Just at the moment of your decision-making to take action toward your new idea, you ambush yourself. The ambush might not cause a rush of amygdala-secreting cortisol and adrenaline, but it might as well be because it can have the same effect. The ambush I'm referring to is your becoming attached to fear-based thoughts. To understand why this can eventually trigger the amygdala, let's return to the importance of the swim-buddy concept, considering one of the most powerful pairs: the thinking-feeling loop.

I like the way Byron Katie, creator of a method of self-inquiry called "The Work" and author of several books, describes thoughts in her book *Loving What Is*: "Thoughts just appear. They come out of nothing and go back to nothing, like clouds moving across the empty sky. They come to pass, not stay. There is no harm in them until we attach to them as if they were true." Once we attach to a thought, we associate a feeling with it. For example, I am floating in warm Hawaiian water with thoughts of relaxation, warmth, and tranquility. The feelings of comfort, peace, and calm relax me, causing my body to secrete the feel-good hormone serotonin. I seek to stay afloat as I focus on breathing and enjoying every moment of peace. I am loving the moment as my body and mind relax.

In that example, I am making a personal leadership decision—leading myself to relaxation. I am concentrating on attaching to these wonderful thoughts that generate corresponding feelings of joy and peacefulness. I want to stress this point to you—in this moment, *I am making the decision* about what thoughts I want to attach to.

Let's consider a second example: Me again, floating in exactly the same body of Hawaiian crystal-blue warm water, but now I'm thinking about the most recent shark attack in this area. My mind races to answer. *What kind of shark was it? A tiger shark, I think. What time of day do they feed? How close to shore do they come? What island had the last shark attack? Maui! Wait, I'm on Maui! What side of the island? West side. Hey, that's the side of the island I'm on right now! Get out of the water now!*

In the second example, guess what kind of ambush is happening to me? If you guess an amygdala ambush, you are correct. What triggered the ambush? Me! I ambushed myself. I attached to a thought and then kept attaching to more thoughts, and what kind of feelings got generated? Fear-based ones. What triggers the amygdala? Fear!

Thoughts are harmless to us until we decide to embrace them. The moment we embrace—or *attach to*—a thought, we give it energy, and that energy comes from a thought and feeling connecting. The end result is an emotion, which we already discussed—it's energy in motion.

That was a simple example. Now let's use a more goal-oriented example—the new-idea example.

New Idea Scenario 1

Over weeks of experiencing a product that I use all the time, I realize that this product can be improved. I think of how to improve this product. My mind races to building a new brand that can help people. I get excited about the idea of helping people and dream about what it would be like when people rave about how my new product helped them. I decide to carve out thirty minutes after dinner every night to work on my innovation. There are so many things I don't know, but I'm certain I can figure it out. I know there's a lot a work ahead, but I keep thinking about how fulfilling it is for me to work on building something new that can help others. I start working longer hours on it. I kiss my kids good night, and as I do, I find more inspiring thoughts of making my kids proud because I am going after a dream—exactly what I want them to do when they get older. My thoughts and feelings continue to spiral upward even when I am presented with inevitable setbacks. I persevere.

New Idea Scenario 2

Over weeks of experiencing a product I use all the time, I realize this product can be improved. I see the improvement immediately, so quickly in fact that I say to myself, *Why hasn't anyone else thought of this? It's too obvious*, I think, and say to myself, *Someone is probably already working on it*, so I decide not take any action.

A few more weeks pass. The current product is beginning to annoy me even more because I know it can be better. I revisit my reasoning and wonder, *What if I built a better product?* As I start to daydream, I "reason" with myself, *That's ridiculous. I haven't gone to school and learned how to build a better product—I can't do that.* Again, I pass on taking any action toward building a new product.

A few months pass and I notice while shopping that there is no product on the market that solves the problem I see. I think again, *What if I actually built it?* Then I think about start-ups that go bankrupt and their founders who lose their houses and get sued, and I bet they even lost their friends and were run out town because they made headlines in the local newspapers. I get a jolt of dread throughout my body. I cringe at the thought of losing everything and telling my wife we have to sell the house. I decide I can deal with the less-than-perfect product and stop thinking about improving that product. I attach to the thoughts *I cannot build this product, and even if I did, I will most likely not be successful.*

▶•◀

This second new-idea scenario was mine for years. I have a sketchbook full of ideas that other inventors brought to market years later. I talked myself out of lots of good ideas because I led myself to connecting with thoughts and consequently feelings that generated emotions that moved me to not go after those ideas. I had created the idea for the Perfect Pushup in 1995 on a submarine mission. (I spent upward of fifty days on a submarine and had long periods of time that I needed to keep myself occupied. Besides working out, I learned to type and sketched ideas in a notebook.) It was not until after I'd worked at a series of civilian jobs after the military that I decided it was worth the risk to try to bring a new idea to market. It was only after four years and two failed companies that I brought Perfect Pushup to market. The reason the Perfect Pushup exists is because I learned to attach to thoughts that were helpful in propelling me (and my team!) forward instead of ambushing me into quitting or not even trying.

I can give you scenario after scenario of attaching to thoughts that are either helpful or hurtful, from writing a book to trying out for a team to not applying to a school because I didn't think I was good enough. The thoughts we connect with start a snowball effect of energy production that can propel us forward, make us turn around, or stop us in our tracks (i.e., fight, flight, or freeze). The thinking-feeling loop can either spin you forward or backward, depending on which thought you decide to embrace.

Be aware of your thoughts. Over time, the actions you take determine your direction. Remember: My singular focus in sharing this knowledge is help you take the *next* action toward your success—it is the next action that matters. There is no need to worry about a series of future actions. I want you to focus on just the *next* helpful action you can take.

EXERCISE | **Hurtful or Helpful?**

Here is a simple exercise I want you to practice now and until your last breath. It involves asking yourself (and your teammates) a very simple question: "Is this thought helpful or hurtful to what I am/we are trying to accomplish?"

My boys hear me asking them this question all the time, especially when they are expressing some E-Motions such as "I am no good at this," "My team sucks," "I'm not going to early morning practice because other teammates aren't either," or "Why should I be the only one working so hard?"

My response to these and so many more E-Motions is asking them, "Boys, is that thought helpful or hurtful [toward helping you achieve your goal]?" I say it so frequently to them, the question is now abbreviated: "Helpful or hurtful?" Of course, they don't really get it at that moment because they are already ambushing themselves. Their amygdala is firing because, before they voiced their frustration to me, they had spent time attaching to thoughts that generated powerful negative emotions. By the time their thoughts reach me, they are already in full fight/flight/freeze mode.

In the early days of parenting, I would engage immediately with them to attempt to get them to see a different point of view. And most of the time, I failed miserably because once the amygdala has hijacked your prefrontal cortex, it can take up to twenty minutes for its nitro-boosting hormones to flush through your body. During that time, I have found the best thing is to let them move through those E-Motions as quickly as possible by getting them to express how they feel (e.g., having a yelling contest) or helping them move their emotions through physical exercise (e.g., pillow punching or wrestling). If you don't move the energy, it will stay with you until you do. Once their venting has peaked is when I typically ask them, "Helpful or hurtful?"

This process of awareness of the thoughts you are attaching to is an important Unstoppable action. I promise you there are opportunities every day for you to practice this—seek them out and boldly ask yourself, friends, family members, or teammates: "Helpful or hurtful?" Building this habit of asking yourself this question will help you avoid spending your precious energy attaching to a thought that will generate hurtful E-Motions that will derail you from accomplishing your dreams.

6 Opening Your CAN of Whoop-Ass

By now you have a general understanding of how potent thoughts are to our success. Let's level up and discuss how to build Unstoppable thoughts on demand by "opening your CAN." First, a quick refresher: there are three kinds of thoughts—past, future, and present. If we attach to negative thoughts in the past, we will experience E-Motions that lead to depression. When we connect to negative thoughts in the future, we will experience E-Motions of anxiety. Depression and anxiety result from negative attachments. This chapter is about helping create and attach to high-performance thoughts in the present while preventing attachment to past or future negative thoughts from impacting your present performance.

Now, remember the Unstoppable Exercise "Play the Opposite Game" from chapter four, where I noted that there is *always* a positive to a negative? So what happens when you play the opposite game with negative thoughts from the past and/or future? You will learn to prevent yourself from sliding down the slippery slopes of depression or anxiety because you will find the opposite thoughts to each hurtful thought, which in turn will lead you to dramatically improving your performance in the present.

Of course, it takes practice to do this, and I want to share a tool that can help you succeed at turning your thoughts into high performing ones. Here's a brief Navy SEAL story to give you the background on how I came up with the tool that I call "opening your CAN."

Before every Navy SEAL mission, the platoon commander and his chief petty officer (the senior enlisted man) perform a platoon inspection. No two missions are the same, and because each person has different responsibilities in the platoon, it's vital to ensure everyone has the mission critical gear needed to carry out the mission. The inspection process requires the senior leaders of the platoon (platoon commander and chief) to visually inspect guns, medical equipment, radios, demolition gear, night vision goggles, and so on. The inspection can take a while and is sometimes mundane, especially if a teammate has forgotten something and they have to run back to get the missing item and start the inspection again.

The military equipment is obviously important, but there is one piece of equipment that is more important than all the others, and I would ask every one of my platoon mates every time if they had it: "their can." I learned about inspecting for their "can" from my very first chief, a senior chief petty officer who was an old-school SEAL. He would often pull me aside and say, "Sir, all these new electronic toys are distracting. I don't want the platoon to rely on these things because they can break, and then what?"

I remember looking at him quizzically and slowly saying, "Ahh, okay, so what do you want them to use, Senior Chief?"

He didn't miss a beat as he looked at me and said, "Sir, no mission ever goes as planned. I want to make sure every one of our boys has their can of whoop-ass with them."

The analogy of the "can of whoop-ass" from SEAL Team is something I have carried forward and modified over the past twenty-five years. It is great to be fired up and focused on what you need to do, but it's even more helpful to direct the energy by attaching to a series of thoughts and actions that will help you perform at your highest level. I call this technique "Opening Your CAN." I have made an acronym out of the word *CAN*: concentrate, activate, and narrow.

The process of Opening Your CAN requires you to attach to positive thoughts that have happened in your past and those that you want to happen in your future. I will start with a simple sports-related example from my son Charlie's water polo club. Charlie was a high school water polo goalie. (He now plays for one of the top D1 college programs in the country, USC.) One of the most difficult roles for a water polo goalie is blocking five-meter penalty shots. These penalty shots are just like the ones in soccer (or *fútbol*), where the shooter is directly in front of the goalie, waiting to take a shot upon the referee's whistle. In soccer, the shooter is using his or her feet, while in water polo, the shooter is treading water and using his or her arm to throw the ball. Blocking 5m shots can completely swing the momentum of the game and definitely impact the shooter's confidence. (Typically, the one taking the 5m shots is the best shooter on the team; if a goalie can block his or her shot, then quite often that shooter's confidence is impacted throughout the rest of the game.)

During his sophomore and junior years, Charlie was well known for his 5m blocks. His blocking average was close to an astounding 50 percent, which is a very helpful statistic when a water polo match goes into a shootout. Again, like soccer, if a water polo game is tied at the end of regulation (it depends on the tournament; some do an overtime period before going to a shootout), a five-person shootout results. Whichever team scores the most points wins the game. Blocking 5m shots in overtime is the difference maker.

Up until senior year, every overtime shootout that Charlie participated in, he would block 5m shots. His coach would often tell me,

"If we are tied going into the last minute, and Charlie is in goal, then I would rather just get to the shootout, because I know he will block the shots needed to win." And most of the time, Charlie did just that, until halfway through his senior season, when he didn't.

I could see he was getting frustrated with himself for not blocking 5m shots. I asked his coach if I could do a series of talks to their team about building an Unstoppable Mindset, and he readily agreed. Each session before practice, I talked to the boys about the things we can control—thoughts, focus, and beliefs—and then how to make them work for us when it matters most. The one habit I worked with each of them on was how to fill up and open their CAN. I used Charlie as an example as I said, "Boys, do you think it is helpful or hurtful for Charlie to be thinking about the last 5m he missed?"

I got a mumbled response: "Hurtful."

I kept pressing. "What would be a helpful thought for him to focus on when preparing for a 5m?"

Silence for a moment and then Charlie said, "Focusing on the last one I blocked."

"*Yes!*" I exclaimed and continued looking at Charlie. "Chow [his nickname], when you look at the 5m shooter, is it helpful or hurtful to think about how good that shooter is and how you haven't blocked any of his shots so far?"

Chow looked at me and said in a monotone voice, "Hurtful."

"Team, what is the more helpful thought you want Charlie thinking about when going up against a 5m shooter?"

One by one, they gave responses such as, "I'm going to block his shot," "Stuff him!" "Be a brick wall," "Make him miss."

The little drill I ran the team through using Charlie as the example was about learning to lead your mind into selecting which thoughts from your past and future you want to bring into your present. Once I explained that it's up to them to decide which thoughts they attach to, I introduced them to their CAN.

I introduced you to your CAN through a sports example because sports examples are easily relatable. Hitting the baseball, golf ball, or tennis ball or throwing the winning touchdown are simple analogies of performance, but you can use your CAN for going after other kinds of goals such as creating (and launching) a product, learning a language, giving a presentation, building a company, getting a promotion, or helping a community. The CAN applies to all goals—it may just require more practice and different timelines specific to those goals.

CONCENTRATE ON THE EXPERIENCE YOU WANT

It takes concentration to sift through your past thoughts. In *The Confident Mind*, Dr. Nate Zinsser uses the analogy of being your own movie director. I love that analogy because you are cutting out the scenes (past experiences) you don't want to see again. In Charlie's case, he must edit out the scenes from his 5m "movie" where he missed the block. The movie he wants to create is a series of blocked shots. Then he takes those past blocked-shot scenes and concentrates on replaying those scenes. But it isn't just visualizing them that counts, it is enriching those "movie" scenes with all of the senses of touch, sight, sound, smell, and anything else that helps him envision the movie, making it as lifelike as possible.

Once he has his edited his "5m blocked-shots" movie, he then must replay the movie again and again. This movie is for his own personal viewing, and he can watch it anytime and anywhere, such as when he goes to bed, when he wakes up, in between classes, on the bus to his game, and of course just before preparing for a 5m shooter. The more he replays it, the more he attaches to these thoughts. The more he attaches and generates corresponding E-Motions, the more he is stimulating neurological responses in his body. The more lifelike he makes his movie, the more he is preparing his mind and body to perform just as he is envisioning it. (There are a series of neurological synapses that occur when you do proper envisioning. This is well documented, and if you are interested in reading more on sports psychology, I highly encourage you to read Dr. Zinsser's book *The Confident Mind*.)

The same strategy can be applied for a range of other goals, including building a business. I concentrated on a series of entrepreneurial outcomes that I wanted a starring role in: from a successful launch of a product to earning a spot on the *Inc.* 500. In each case, I would build a series of movie scenes that helped me visualize the next step in achieving my larger goals, such as developing a winning product. I would imagine the team working together, the customer feedback, and even the retailer calls asking for more product. When I wasn't working, I was replaying those specific movie scenes in my mind. I was daydreaming my future all the time. I continue to do the same today with each new goal.

ACTIVATE YOUR BODY

The second step in Opening Your CAN is activating your weapons platform—your body. The best first action here is breathing, specifically, inhaling through your nose. When we inhale through our noses, we initiate a series of additional pulmonary actions that prepare the air for immediate use in our bodies. Not only does the action of intentional inhaling through our nostrils and exhaling through our mouth prepare our body for peak performance, but it helps us concentrate and prevent our amygdala from hijacking our systems.

To perform at our best means we must stay calm and creative, which means we need our prefrontal cortex functioning. To do this means keeping the body replenished with good air while expelling old air (carbon dioxide). As you take three to five deep breaths, watch your movie scenes that you want to experience again. At the end of those initial breaths, it's time to switch from replaying the movie scenes from the past and/or future and narrowing your focus onto the moment.

I also use this breathing technique when getting myself into a creative state of mind. Each time I sat down to sketch product ideas, I found myself going through a little state-change drill. I closed my eyes, took a series of deep slow breaths, and cleared my mind in preparation of opening it up for new ideas. I knew nothing of meditation in those early days living on a submarine. I just knew that switching gears from conducting combat diving missions to creating new products required a clear and focused mind.

NARROW YOUR FOCUS

The final stage of opening your CAN is narrowing your focus. Your mind and body now know exactly what experience you want, your body is alert and prepared, and so now you need to keep your focus solely on the moment of action. Do not think. Just let it happen. Thinking slows down your reaction time. Just be. Let your mind and body do their work together. The key here is eliminating all distractions. The only thought that matters in this moment is staying in the moment. Do not let your mind wander. If it does, quickly replay your movie at double or triple speed. These recalibrations can be done in microseconds.

When it's game time, you can feel it, because your heart rate is getting elevated and your breathing increases to feed your raising pulse. You smile because you know your body is secreting extra hormone energy to help you perform at your peak. These moments are the moments you have trained for, and you're ready to do something extra special. Let your narrowing of focus remind you that nervousness is just fuel for your body to perform at its highest level. You are now ready to Open Your CAN of performance whoop-ass!

Charlie and I performed this drill every night for five nights before his next game. He had not blocked a 5m in six games (typically, he blocked one or two per game). In his next game, he blocked two 5m shots for a convincing win. He finished his senior year season setting a school water polo record for an undefeated league season and winning the league championship.

The routine of opening your CAN is as important as following the steps of concentrate, activate, and narrow. At first, it will seem awkward; your Whiner voice will make fun of your efforts and say things like "You've got to be kidding yourself. This isn't going to work," or "You don't know what you're doing." You wouldn't believe how many times I told myself, *Stop sketching. You suck at drawing. Why do you think you can create a new product? You nearly flunked out of engineering classes at the Naval Academy. Do you know how long this is going to take to get built? You don't even have any money to build one of these products.* Blah, blah, blah, and blah. Do not give the Whiner an ounce of your energy.

As mentioned before, I am a visual learner, and when I set off to do something I often create pictures in my mind. When it comes to learning how not to listen to the Whiner, I think of a little furry gremlin with a face that looks like it's smelling sour milk. It has no teeth or claws. It's a fat, sloth-like, snot-nosed, drool-dripping, weasel-voiced character that I will grab by the scruff of its neck and chuck into an old steam trunk (like the ones used by passengers on the *Titanic*—I often think of sending that character down with the *Titanic*!). There are times I don't pick up the Whiner but instead give it a swift kick like shooting the game-winning penalty shot in soccer. Of course, the Whiner keeps coming back, and that is his role—to be our early-detection system to alert us that we are about to do something we have never done before. Think of the Whiner as if it's our proverbial canary in the coal mine, constantly looking out for danger. Of course, the Whiner is not all bad; there are some times when the danger is real and we need to pay attention. The Whiner only knows what it knows and likes the comfort of familiarity, which is where mediocrity lives. I have explained several ways to deal with the Whiner in chapter four, but when it comes to opening your CAN, there is another technique I want to share: making state changes.

STATE CHANGES

When working on a submarine, I found it very hard to flip from the daily frogman duties to the dream state of a future entrepreneur. I started intentional routines that allowed me to transition from one state of mind to the next. These state changes were not just mental but also physical. For instance, once my SEAL duties were complete, I conducted a workout. Typical workouts on a submarine are cramped and require some creativity and scheduling around other submariners and their duties. I used my workout not only to stay fit but also to clear my mind from a military focus to a creative one. The first portion of the workout was replaying what we'd practiced that day. The second portion of the workout involved a slow and gradual transition to thinking of things to invent. Of course, the transitions did not always go smoothly. On tougher SEAL training days, I spent much more time replaying how we could have performed better. The point is that physical exercise is an excellent way to activate your mind in preparation for whatever you seek to focus on next.

I created transitions from SEAL work to creative work that involved not only a physical workout but also physical actions such as a change of clothes and location. I had selected a specific table in the back of a room where I faced the wall so that if anyone entered the room, they saw my back. I wanted to limit eye contact with other people to avoid casual conversations. I needed to be completely focused on creating my future. To help deter people from bothering me, I put on a headset and played some music (softly). And there I would sit for a couple of hours at a time drawing/sketching all kinds of ideas. I didn't appreciate my routine at the time or the physiological effects of what I was doing. I just knew that this process allowed me to concentrate on creativity, activate my body, and narrow my focus to dramatically improve my ability to attach and create future thoughts that I wanted to experience.

Years later, that sketchbook would produce an idea that led to an award-winning business plan at Carnegie Mellon University's business school and acted as the foundation for the products we created to reach the top of the *Inc.* 500 list of fastest-growing companies. Whether your goal is to perform at the highest athletic levels or build the most wildly creative products or any number of other goals, learning to use state changes will help you open your CAN of peak performance to achieve your goals. We *all* have a CAN of Whoop-Ass inside of us. All we need to do is practice unleashing it!

When I use the term *state changes*, I am referring to the specific act of engaging not only your mind but also your body, like a one-two punch combination to an opponent (in this case, your opponent is that little Whiner gremlin in your head). The basic premise behind a state change is shifting your energy and focus from one activity to another that also involves activating your body. Here's a simple state change: going from sitting down to standing up. The act of standing up requires you to focus on engaging a series of muscles along with paying attention to your surroundings, such as by keeping your balance while not bumping into something. Here are more complex state changes: shifting from working on a spreadsheet to playing the piano or from answering emails to painting or from reading to walking in the woods. The most effective state changes involve all your intelligence centers (mental, emotional, and spiritual) along with your physical center (body).

There are countless ways for you to perform a state change. These are a few that help me transition from detaching from one thought/action process to another: working out, walking my dog, moving work from one room to another, taking a shower, having a cup of coffee, listening to my favorite music, walking around the block, doing ten push-ups, taking five deep breaths with my eyes closed, reading a fiction book, cleaning my desk or closet. Some of these I need time to perform; others I can do sitting in an airplane seat.

Find a few state-change activities that will work for you. The purpose of the state change is to disrupt and disengage your thought-feeling loop so you can refocus on something else. I completely understand how hard it can be to detach from a negative thought. Use a state change to activate all your thinking/feeling centers to help you switch gears. The first step to success in detaching from negative thought patterns is being aware you are in one in the first place. Once you are aware of it, then making the state change is easy to do. Make a list of your favorite activities and think of ways to incorporate them into your day. Giving yourself a state change is like treating yourself to your favorite drink or snack. You can use your own state changes several times a day, and I encourage you to schedule them throughout your day. The process of calendaring your state changes gives you something to look forward to, which will keep your mindset positive.

GIVING THE HEISMAN TO POOR PERFORMANCE

State changes are not only useful for dealing with transitions from one mental activity to the next, such as from working on math problems to writing, but they are also extremely helpful when your performance is not going as planned. Let's turn to another sports analogy. You are golfing with friends in a local tournament on a course you play all the time. You routinely shoot eighty-five on this course, but today your shots are all over the place, and you start thinking, *I'll be lucky to break a hundred.* Your teammates start wondering aloud if they picked the wrong person for their foursome. They make their negative comments wrapped in jokes, but you know they aren't happy with your subpar performance.

The more frustrated you get, the worse you play. What started out as an event you were looking forward to all week is now something you're no longer enjoying. You are angry at yourself, questioning your equipment (*Are these the right clubs for me?*), and annoyed by your friends' comments. You finish with one of your worst scores in over a year and are seriously thinking about giving up your golf membership. After all, this is supposed to be an activity you enjoy, so why continue doing it if you don't enjoy it?

If you've ever played golf, I think you can relate to this example. If you cannot, then think of any activity you've done over and over again successfully that then, when it counts, you fail to perform. When these failures occur, and they will, I want you to take a deep breath, think up your favorite state change, and say, "This is *not* me." There are lots of reasons why you will not perform well on any given day. I suspect I could write an entire book with reasons why I choked, failed, whiffed, missed, or just plain made a mistake.

The fact of the matter is sh-t happens to all of us. The key question is how to handle poor performance. Are you going to remain attached to your mistakes, replay them again and again, while generating more miserable emotions to the point that every time you see a golf course you get a negative emotion swelling up inside of you as if to say, "I hate that sport"? *No!* You are not, because you are going to follow this simple process for getting your performance back on track and your attitude in check to keep opening your CAN of Whoop-Ass.

Before I share the process, please remember this: we are human, we aren't perfect, and we make mistakes. Accept these truths as part of the process of recovering from your mistakes. It has often been said, "Champions have short-term memories." True champions do not focus on their past mistakes. The more you focus on a past mistake, the more you bring the past into your present, which can doom your performance to repeating mistakes in the future. When mistakes happen—and they *will* happen—the trick is treating them like a cloud that floats by harmlessly overhead.

NOT Me!

The NOT Me! technique is a strategy you can use to break that loop and prevent yourself from repeating past mistakes. While it is true that champions don't dwell on their mistakes and keep their focus on the next action they'll take, their thought process is a little more specific than just "having short-term memory." In my view, champions have *selective* memory. When they make mistakes, they do not simply forget about them. They coach themselves to move past the mistakes. The best champions in whatever field of sport, business, art, military, or any other arena you choose know that focusing on the mistake is not helpful.

That's the starting point, but then they must be their own best coaches. They attach to their internal Winner voice by being kind to themselves. They coach themselves through the process of not giving the mistake any more energy and instead keeping themselves focused on the very next action. Building an Unstoppable Mindset comes with being your own best friend. Your mind, body, and even your spirit will respond so much better to positive versus negative reinforcement.

Remember: The single most important leadership role you have is leading yourself, and the mindset required when you make a mistake involves leading how you think and feel. You must learn to be kind to yourself. Another way to look at this is by asking yourself, *Hey, is it helpful or hurtful to make myself feel bad for missing that shot?* Pretend for a moment you're coaching yourself. Answer that question—helpful or hurtful? You know the answer; it's hurtful. All it does is add more pressure to your next action, compounding the odds of making another mistake. Instead, you want to reduce the pressure on yourself by lowering the stakes of your next action. Break down the action into smaller chunks and find something positive about each next action you take so you can find small wins that will build upon each other. The key to this is first stopping the process of taking actions that are not helpful to your success. This is why I created the acronym NOT Me! with inspiration from Dr. Nate Zinsser's book *The Confident Mind*. (I have long used NOT Me! but I love how Dr. Zinsser details three specific traits: Temporary, Non-representative, and One-off. I have built a memory combining his words with my acronym of NOT Me!) I want you to use it to coach yourself into not repeating a past mistake and move on to performing at your potential. NOT Me! stands for:

- **Not** representative of what I can do;
- **One-off** action that is not normal of the actions I take; and
- **Temporary** mistake that will not last because my next action will be better.

"NOT Me!" is what I want you to say every time you make a mistake that you don't want to repeat. Essentially, the mistake you made was not your best. Therefore, it's *not* you—it is not representative of who are you or what you are capable of. The mistake was nothing more than a cosmic speedbump, a blip, an aberration, a hiccup in time that just reminds you that you are human and imperfect. That's all; nothing more, nothing less. You will learn from the mistake later, but at this moment in the middle of your performance, sweep it to the side and get back to performing at your best. NOT Me! is a powerful yet simple coaching mantra that you can repeat to yourself to keep yourself calm and relaxed.

And why is it important to stay calm and relaxed? Because if you don't, your amygdala fires, which will be like throwing gasoline on your little mistake and turning that mistake into a full-blown three-alarm blaze. When this happens, your amygdala hijacks your ability to perform at your best because now you are no longer loose, relaxed, and open to taking what comes. Instead you are tense, tight, and closed-minded.

Back to the not-so-fictitious golf scenario. You take your first few shots, and they're terrible. You shoot three over par on the first hole. You stop, smile, laugh to yourself, and say, "This is NOT you. Relax, my friend. We are playing this game to enjoy the day." You walk over to a friend, compliment him on his first hole, and tell him how much you like playing golf with him. You stop, take three deep breaths, and as you do you play your movie clips of past perfect swings—you hear the crack of the ball against your driver, you feel your back leg pivot as your hips move in the direction of the ball, then you hear your buddies say, "There's the guy I know!"

You finish your breathing while replaying those movie clips a few times. There's a smile on your face. Your shoulders are relaxed. You address the ball and swing without thinking. A moment later, your teammates say something along the lines you envisioned, and a few back slaps later and a happy walk down the fairway, your first hole is a distant memory as you ready yourself to do what you did again.

The only part of that particular story that is fictitious is me shooting a golf score of eighty-five. Other than that, I have lived that movie several times. That is a simple use of NOT Me!—it gets harder when the mistake is longer lasting, like ordering the incorrect amount of Perfect Pushup inventory and nearly putting my company into bankruptcy. Those kinds of mistakes can last a year or longer and can be harder to forget and forgive yourself for.

However, I am here to tell you those mistakes require the same actions as those short-term athletic ones do—they involve coaching yourself to continually remind yourself that the mistake was not representative of me; it was a one-off (I will learn from it and not make it again), and the mistake is temporary—I will come back from it. In essence, the mistake is NOT Me! It is not who I am, nor does it represent who I wish to be in the future.

Using NOT Me! as a reminder—as a mantra—helps ensure that you do not identify yourself with the mistake. Your mistakes do not define you. Instead, how you respond to your mistakes shows the world and yourself who you truly are. To Be Unstoppable doesn't mean you have never been stopped. It means you have been stopped and you know how to keep going, and that is what we are doing here together—learning to Be Unstoppable when we make mistakes and encounter obstacles.

EXERCISE | **Opening Your CAN**

Make a habit of bringing your CAN with you wherever you go. The key action of this habit is practicing opening it every day. You can practice opening your CAN while sitting at your desk, going for a ride in a car (so long as you aren't driving!), taking a break, or going for a walk. Make opening your CAN a routine and watch how your performance will improve over time.

I open my speaking CAN for each new speech literally hundreds of times before I step onstage. Use your CAN to practice certain elements of the actions you seek to improve. You don't always have to practice the entire scene at once; sometimes rehearsing shorter scenes of your entire movie can be just as helpful. Have fun with this. It's your mind to control so give it focus by opening your CAN!

Here's the exercise—Opening Your CAN: Pick a goal you are committed to achieving and develop a CAN for it. Pick out a song for your CAN and listen to it while you close your eyes and develop a sequence of movie scenes that you want to have a starring role in. As you fill your CAN, make sure to include scenes of you performing the necessary work to accomplish your goal. Incorporate every element you can think of to make these scenes feel even more real—the more senses, the better. Each day when you begin working toward your goal, I want you to practice opening your CAN, going through the breathing techniques (state changes) of activating your body, and narrowing your focus on what you need to accomplish in the moment to help you get a step closer to your goal.

What's your goal you are making a CAN for?

List three state changes you will use:

1.

2.

3.

FOCUS
7

One of the most effective tools Navy SEAL instructors use to convince candidates to quit is cold water. The technique they created is called surf torture. It's a very simple exercise: walk into knee-deep water, turn around to face the shore (so you can't see the waves coming), link arms with your teammates, and sit down. During the first couple of weeks of BUD/S, instructors were quite adept at getting students cold enough to walk out of the water and ring the bell. (Ringing the bell three times means you have decided to leave the class or drop out, aka quit.) At the beginning of BUD/S, I was one of three officers in the class. Our senior officer, Bert (a good friend to this day), had been medically dropped two years earlier but was given an invitation to return to BUD/S upon healing. This was his second attempt, and he was quite familiar with surf torture.

"Millsy, here's the deal. They are going to keep us in the surf zone until one of us quits or they get bored—let's hope they have a short attention span."

I looked at him with a half grimace and asked, "And if they don't get bored, then what?"

He responded flatly. "Sing and sun."

"What's that supposed to mean?"

He looked at me as he shrugged his shoulders. "I find it easier to take my mind off the cold by focusing on singing our song and looking at the sun between each wave. The moment we focus on how cold the water is *is* the moment we get ourselves in trouble."

Just as he explained his theory of handling cold water, one of the instructors barked out the order, "Link arms! Forward march!"

We had been lined up shoulder to shoulder along the beach facing the sea. We each linked arms (so we would stay together while getting hit by waves breaking just over our heads when we sat down), and slowly walked into the sixty-degree Pacific Ocean off of Coronado, California. The tide was low, which meant we walked for about twenty-five yards until reaching roughly knee-deep water.

The instructor again barked another command through his electronic megaphone, "Halt!"

We stopped walking and waited for his next instruction.

"Ahhh-bout-face. Link arms. Take seats!" (When you about-face, you automatically unlink arms so you can pivot 180 degrees—in this case, we turned around to face the beach and our torturer, now smiling.)

The moment you sit down on the sandy bottom is the worst part because the initial shock of cold water spilling down your neck takes your breath away. I think that's why the instructor was smiling—he was getting his jollies from watching all of us hyperventilate as our bodies adjusted to the shock of the cold. After a few seconds, most of us got our breathing under control as we started to sing our song, "You're a Grand Old Flag." (Every SEAL class has a class song, and you sing it all the time to help with the tedium of certain challenging evolutions such as long runs, paddles, PT, and especially when being surf tortured.)

At first, it was hard to get the words out while getting control of our breathing and dealing with the crashing waves over our heads every few seconds. After a couple of minutes, Class 181 found a rhythm between each wave and the verses of "You're a Grand Old Flag." Bert was right. I found my focus alternating between singing loud and proud, looking at the sun, and squeezing my teammates' interlocked arms to better handle the cold water. The louder I sang, the warmer I felt. Soon much of the class was belting out the patriotic words to our class song.

Unfortunately, there were a few classmates who could not seem to make the shift from thinking about how cold the water was to focusing on something else. I'm not sure how long we sat there (we were not allowed to wear watches), but one cold classmate decided it was more than he could handle. He broke ranks (unlocked his arms), stood up, walked to the instructor, and quit. Two instructors accompanied the shivering candidate back to the compound.

Mr. Megaphone turned to us and said, "Anyone else want to make the smart decision like Mr. Jones [not his real name]? I'll let you think about it for a little while." We sang our song two or three times more and then received the order to leave the surf zone.

I'm not sure what is worse: the act of getting surf tortured or the anticipation of getting surf tortured. I thought about it constantly for the next twenty-four hours until the instructor made good on his threat and put us back in the water for another round. Once again, he was successful in convincing another candidate that SEAL training was not for him. Except this time, we did not stay in the water nearly as long. Our classmate quit within minutes of our being told to take seats. It was as if he had already decided he was going to quit, but wanted to wait a few minutes in the cold water to think about it.

Over the first couple of weeks, the instructors took turns submerging us in the Pacific Ocean. Eventually, surf torture stopped producing quitters. We had become accustomed to the commands "Link arms. Take seats." We even started making fun of the commands, barking them out to each other during our free time (out of earshot of our instructors, of course). We were making friends with being surf tortured—we no longer feared it. You could hear classmates saying, "It's a sunny day, boys. Let's work on our face tans!" In other words, look at the sun and feel the warmth. We had discovered the trick to surf torture: keep your focus on feeling the warmth, and you will be warm. It's not possible to focus on two things at once. If you keep your focus on being warm, then it is really hard to feel cold.

A week later, surf torture stopped.

We had about two weeks without being surf tortured until the first night of Hell Week.

Hell Week starts on a Sunday evening and goes until Friday afternoon. On average, a BUD/S class gets 3.5 hours of sleep for the entire week. There are three eight-hour shifts of SEAL instructors running the class through drill after drill, from obstacle courses to surf passage to rock portage to PT and, of course, all kinds of twisted cold-water torture. By the time Class 181 had reached Hell Week (during my time, Hell Week started in the sixth of thirty weeks of BUD/S training; today Hell Week starts earlier in training), our class size had dwindled to thirty-four—thirty-three enlisted men and one officer (me). (Sadly, Bert was medically dropped, and the officer, another good friend [Tom], was rolled to class 183.) My first week as class officer, and the only officer in the class, was Hell Week.

During Hell Week's night shift (12:00 a.m.–8:00 a.m.), our lead instructor—Instructor Boston, the short, wiry man with a thick south Boston accent—began with surf torture. However, this was the first time we had been surf tortured at night; there was no sun to look at, only the lights of the rescue vehicles. With an electronic megaphone always at his lips, he led us into the water during high tide, our path illuminated by searchlights from two modified four-by-four trucks.

After issuing the standard surf-torture commands, he walked above the high-water mark into dry sand, squatted down, and used his finger to draw a large X in the sand. He then said, "Here's waht we are gonna do: you are gonna stay in that wahter until one's yah walks out, steps on this here X, and says the magic words, 'I quit!' Once I get my first quittah, then yah can getta outta the wahter!"

The moment he finished, we began singing "You're a Grand Old Flag" to show our resilience. Unfazed, Instructor Boston fired pop flares one after another, walking along the shoreline as veteran visiting Navy SEALs egged him on. (Hell Weeks can act as reunions for older SEALs who get special invitations to come back to witness the newer classes.)

As time passed, Instructor Boston seemed bored, pacing faster along the shore. Then he stopped abruptly as if an idea had just popped into his mind, and he ordered the Navy doctor (Navy protocol requires a medical professional be on-site for every exercise in Hell Week) to park his ambulance near him. After parking the ambulance, Boston asked the doc to open up the back of the vehicle. When the doc opened the back doors, a huge plume of heat steamed out of the truck. We all saw it and what looked like a little candle of light flickering inside—it looked so warm and inviting that we literally stopped singing for a beat.

Instructor Boston, seizing the opportunity, asked Doc to teach us about hypothermia. As Doc explained the clinical definition, Boston cut him off, asking how long we'd have to be in the water to become hypothermic. According to Doc's chart, it would take 19.5 minutes in the 58.4-degree water. Boston exaggeratedly checked his watch, noting we'd been in for over twenty-five minutes. He eagerly asked Doc to list the symptoms of hypothermia.

At that moment, we stopped singing and intently listened to the conversation between our tormentor and the medical expert. As the doctor described the first symptom of hypothermia, uncontrollable shaking, we immediately began to shiver. Our panic grew when he mentioned memory loss.

"You might forget your teammates' names," the doc cautioned, which led us to frantically question each other's names.

"What's my name!" we shouted to each other.

Instructor Boston then asked, "Doc, what happens if they stay in the water longah?" to which the doctor replied, "You could die."

The SEAL instructor smiled as he held the megaphone up to the doctor's mouth and said, "Doc, say that again!"

Doc cleared his throat and said firmly, "You. Could. Die."

Boston then turned to us and said, "Come on, guys. Yah really wantta die for this? Yah know whatta I got in thah ambulance?" He waited a moment before responding to his own question: "I got hot cocoa!"

Upon hearing this, Petty Officer Smith (not his real name) broke ranks, walked out of the water, and stepped right on the X Boston had drawn in the sand.

Boston's conversation could be heard through his megaphone: "Petty Officer Smith, why are you out of the wahta?"

Smith, shaking uncontrollably, replied, "I wanna some hot cocoa."

Boston looked at him and asked the same question again. This time Smith slowly and quietly said, "I quit."

Boston then patted Smith on the back and said, "Don't worry about it. This ain't for everyone. I don't blame yah!" He then ordered two SEALs to escort him to X-Division.

Then Instructor Boston walked into the water about knee deep and asked us a question: "Class 181, listen to me very clearly: Did I say I had hot cocoa for quitters?" He paused to let his statement sink in. "Do yah think yah get sumthing fah quittin? Yah think there's hot cocoa on the battlefield!"

He waited another moment before nearly shouting, "You get nuthin'! If yah lucky, you have each other and yah ability to focus on getting the mission done—that's it! Now, I got my first quittah, so you can get out of the wahter—just long enough for this doc to check yah out. Then yah gonna go back in, 'cause I want more quittahs. Welcome to Hell Week, Class 181!"

Hell Week had begun, and it was up to us to find the strength within ourselves and in our teammates to endure the punishment and persevere. The most powerful weapon we would learn to use to our advantage was how to control our focus.

FOCUS FUNNEL 101

As Instructor Half Butt had foreshadowed just weeks earlier, his job and the job of his instructors was to create that conversation in our heads to lead us to make a decision—to choose if we could or could not do something. Thoughts start the process, but focus propels those thoughts into action.

I shared that surf-torture story not to help prepare you for learning how to sit in cold water for long periods of time but to instead illustrate the power of focus. It turned out that all of us were hypothermic throughout different periods of Hell Week. One of us got as low as eighty-nine degrees. (He had very little body fat and was made to sit in the rewarming facility—a hot tub—not a fun experience. I would much rather just stay cold!) The instructors represented a cast of characters I nicknamed Instructor Psycho, Aloha, Ogre, and Antichrist. All of them took different approaches to exactly the same thing: attempting to shift our focus to the pain of the situation in the moment.

You may be saying to yourself, *That's a great story, Alden, but I'm never going through SEAL training, so this doesn't really apply to me.* Oh yes, it does. Because our focus determines our direction. It doesn't matter if your mission is to sit in cold water or pass math class or muster enough energy to try again at going after your goal. Our focus is the difference maker. It's how we attach to a thought and give that thought energy.

It is very important to understand how focus works. The better you understand the power of one of your most important weapons for success, the more prepared you will be to take control of it when your focus drifts (remember: We are human, we are imperfect, and so our focus *will* drift). Focus acts like a funnel. It funnels energy that drives us to take an action.

Our focus funnel is one of the very few things we can control (remember: Thoughts and beliefs are our other two mindset controllables). The harder we focus on something, the more intensely we give that thought energy. For example, when we were sitting in cold water focused on singing our song in unison and in pitch (sort of), we were not focused on the plight of our cold-water submersion. Sure, our bodies were cold, but that was not where our focus was. Though there were only a few square inches of skin on our cheeks that could register the warmth of the sun, as long as I kept my focus on that warmth, I did not "feel" the cold water all around my body. Of course, my body was registering the cold water, but my brain was too busy focusing on the sun. Take away the sun, stop singing, and bring

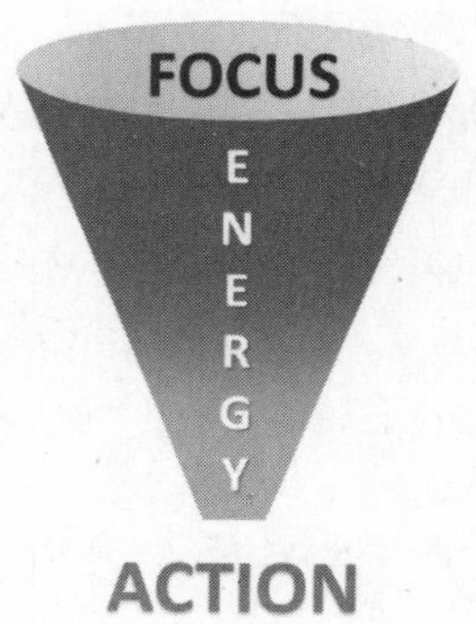

a medical professional to tell you what you should be experiencing, and guess what happens if you focus on that. You experience it! You can be hypothermic in a ninety-degree tub if you focus on it hard enough (not to mention staying in there for a while).

Focus is how we attach to a thought. Remember: Thoughts are neither helpful nor hurtful until we FOCUS on them. In the case of surf torture, the moment you focus on how cold you are is the moment you are in trouble. You learn the power of your focus quickly in SEAL training. Most of us will not have this kind of training in our lives, so we must learn how to practice. The reason focus is so important is that your focus will help you keep taking action toward your goal, whereas focus on the wrong things will stop you in your tracks. There are three critical aspects I want you to know about our focus funnel.

Focus Rule 1—The Focus Funnel Is Agnostic

Our focus funnel doesn't care what kind of thought we put in it. We can put a helpful thought or a hurtful thought. The focus funnel doesn't care. You're in control of your focus funnel, and you must be ever vigilant as to what kind of thoughts you put into it. Our focus funnel is a tool, and it's waiting for our command of how to use it.

Focus Rule 2—The Focus Funnel Is a Magnet

Whatever thought you decide to focus on attracts other similar thoughts. These similar thoughts act like a magnet, and we'll begin to seek more thoughts to support the ones that we are focusing on. If you aren't careful, you will seek other people with the same focus. This can cut both ways. Find people focused on succeeding, and your focus will match theirs. Conversely, find people focused on deciding something cannot be done, and if you aren't careful, you start sharing their focus on all the reasons something cannot be achieved.

Focus Rule 3—The Focus Funnel Has an Important Structure

Our focus develops energy by how strong the walls of our funnels are. If we don't allow outside distractions in, then our focus funnels channel all our energy toward that thought, building a strong attachment to it. When this happens, we are taking committed actions—we're all in, using our full agency, and our focus is strong. When the walls of our funnels are porous, some of our energy flows out of the sides, and the resulting energy is less committed, and the action taken is weaker. Getting "laser focused" is to have your focus funnel so strong that the resulting energy comes out in laser-like form.

▸•◂

Of course, there's no such thing as funnels inside our skulls capturing key thoughts and generating energy that enables us to produce laser-like focus. However, I always find it helpful to have a visual understanding of something so we can build our own movies around what we want and how we can achieve it. In the case of our focus, there is one challenge that we all have to deal with: holes in our funnels. Since we don't have a titanium funnel in our heads, we have to practice using our focus funnels, in particular, learning how to strengthen them. As mentioned in Focus Rule 3, our funnels can be porous. These holes can come from lots of different places, both outside and from within (see image on page 158).

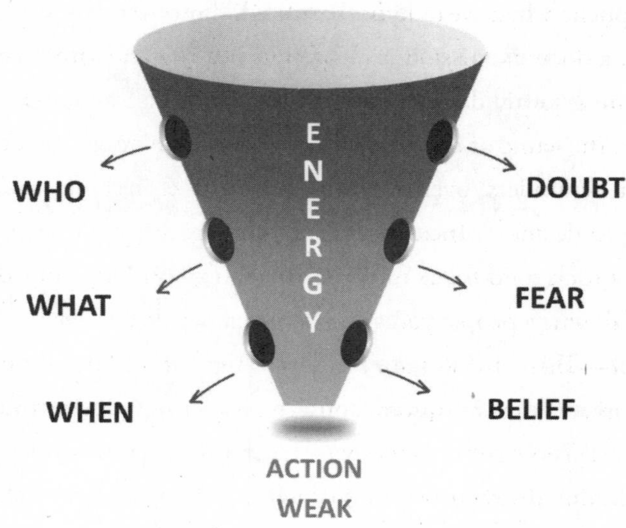

External Hole Makers

There are lots of external hole makers that can impact our focus funnels. I break these into three basic groups of who, what, and when.

Who—Remember the old adage "one bad apple spoils the bunch"? The same goes for one bad focus from a friend, colleague, teammate, or family member. Who you spend time with impacts your focus if you aren't careful. The saying "you are the company you keep" is another way of saying your focus will become the focus of those around you. It is one of the reasons there is a place in BUD/S called X-Division. This is the place where all those people who have decided not to continue with BUD/S are put. They are not allowed to interact with candidates still in training because instructors are acutely aware of how quickly negativity (a type of focus) can spread.

Then there are people in positions of power or known experts who want to impact your focus. Think back to the doctor telling us what happens when we're hypothermic. Who doesn't trust a doctor? After all, a doctor's mission is to keep us healthy and safe. I certainly was listening to my doctor when he said, "Lead a less-active lifestyle and learn the game of chess." Thanks to my mom's positive focus and continual reminders, over time my focus funnel became stronger on deciding to do more. Incidentally, my hope is this book inspires you to build a rock-solid focus funnel focused on achieving your dreams. Be careful which people you allow to influence your focus.

What—There are so many things vying for our attention at any given moment. Our brains are constantly scanning our surroundings for threats. Remember: Negativity bias is our survival mechanism, and our brains always prioritize surviving over anything else. The simplest way to illustrate the power of negativity bias is to turn on the news. The large majority of all reported news is negative. Negativity makes people pay attention, and paying attention is exactly what news stations want you to do. In the business of news, negativity sells.

Negativity is at the top of the what group, but, of course, there are other hole makers here such as the internet, TV, video games, magazines, movies, cell phones—the list of distractions goes on. There are so many different things that can distract you from your focus at any given moment. I can get so easily distracted that I will sometimes put a blanket or a towel over my head and computer monitor when I write. It's my way of creating a make-believe force field for my focus funnel. It sounds crazy, but the act of doing that makes me feel more focused on what I am writing and helps me get into the writing zone faster.

When—There are times of day that can seriously impact your ability to focus. I find my focus is strongest first thing in the morning. Sleep allows my brain to rest and dump the useless information it collected throughout the last day. If I have to do something that requires intense focus (e.g., writing, inventing, creating), I typically schedule those activities for the morning. Of course, that doesn't always work, and that's okay because I have learned to turn my focus on when I really need it.

The other hole-making time you want to watch for is when your focus is naturally drifting. Perhaps you have just eaten a big meal, and your stomach is requiring more blood flow for digestion. It can be hard to concentrate during that time. Or maybe you have been focused for so long that you notice it is becoming harder and harder to concentrate. You are starting to slow down. You are having a harder time performing tasks. This is normal.

We need to take breaks from focusing too. It's almost as if our funnel gets too hot from all the energy we are generating from it, and it slowly starts to lose shape. When focus drifts, it's time to shift it—to give it a rest. Reread the section in chapter six regarding state changes; this intentional change in activities will give your focus funnel time to cool down and reenergize.

Internal Hole Makers

There is really only one internal hole maker—fear. Fear has many faces, from doubt to shame to guilt to embarrassment and beyond, all of which we can find shifting our focus from taking action to giving up. Here are the three major ones.

Doubt—The number one hole maker we will battle all our lives is doubting whether we can do something. Doubt is fear's favorite weapon to stop us from even trying. When we question ourselves, we are reducing our focus, removing energy from giving it our all. Sometimes, that doesn't impact our performance. Other times it becomes the difference maker. Doubt leads our focus to attach to other thoughts making us wonder if we have enough resources or if we are ready or if we are going to look stupid. Doubt is an insidious focus-funnel wrecking ball and can dramatically reduce our focus in seconds if we aren't on guard for this fearmonger. For example, doubt was the main driver for the large majority of my classmates to not pass the PT test following Instructor Half Butt's conversation in front of the Creature. Doubt was also behind my fifteen years of procrastination for not pursuing ideas I had sketched while serving on a submarine or the ten years it took me to write my first book.

Insecurity—When we are insecure, we are scared; we are not sure of ourselves and we fear failing, embarrassment, and just plain thinking about "looking stupid in front of others." Insecurity can funnel off precious all-in, can-do goal achievement energy and then produce the failing results we feared in the first place. Insecurity can act like our own self-fulfilling prophecy that supports our initial fear-based thoughts that we cannot achieve our goal. The irony of overcoming our natural insecurities around trying something new, of taking a risk, leads us to greater joy when we overcome an obstacle. The confidence received from the sense of accomplishment of attaining a goal we have never done can propel us to pursue even greater goals and embrace more uncertainty. Most of the time, the single greatest obstacle we must overcome is not the external challenge that our goals provide, but the internal struggle of shifting our focus away from what we think cannot be done and instead keeping our focus funnels fixed on *how* we can do it.

Beliefs—When we attach to a thought, we give it energy by focusing on it. The way we keep giving energy to a thought is by looking for reasons to support our thoughts. We are thought-making machines, and the more we support a thought, the more we believe that thought. When we embrace a thought, such as *I missed that free throw in the basketball game. Therefore I am not good at making free throws*, we will look to prove to ourselves that our judgment about ourselves is correct. Once this supported thought—aka a belief—takes root in our brains, we start enabling the corresponding thought with more support. In the next basketball game, our new belief becomes a self-fulfilling prophecy as we step up to the free throw line to take the shot. We are telling ourselves again and again what we expect to happen—*I am not good at making free throws.*

What typically happens next is exactly what you might expect—you miss the shot. If you keep feeding this belief, it can grow into a much more powerful stopping force. Over time, you might reason next that you aren't any good at the game of basketball and decide you should stop playing the sport. You could then rationalize that you do not perform well under pressure because all free throws have an element of pressure associated with them. Therefore, you should only seek jobs that avoid putting any pressure on you. This is an example of a limiting belief, and it can make massive, energy-depleting holes in your funnel. I spend the entire next chapter discussing beliefs because they are the controllable that can help us Be Unstoppable. Not all beliefs are limiting. Beliefs can empower; an empowering belief can give us laser-like focus to persevere through the most challenging of times.

In chapter two, you saw an illustration of the basic leadership decision we all must make in our pursuit of a dream. The decision in its simplest form is deciding "I can" or "I can't." As Instructor Half Butt would say, "Ain't complicated. It's just hard." And he's right. It is hard to lead yourself to make the decision (i.e., attach to the thought) that you can do something that you have never done before. Between your external and internal focus-funnel hole makers, your leadership wheel of decision doesn't seem so simple anymore. I visualize it looking something like this (and even this picture is incomplete).

I often think of the arrow on the wheel as our focus funnel. Our thoughts are whirling by just like that wheel in the game show *Wheel of Fortune*, except there is one difference. In the game show, the wheel stops by luck. The mindset decision wheel in our heads is within our control. We decide where we want it to stop and which thought we want to enter into our focus funnel. My point of reminding you of this concept is that you decide how to lead yourself. This is challenging because we are faced with all kinds of distractions that can sway us to make decisions that will change our direction. What I have found over time is we also have control over how many thoughts we want to put on our leadership decision wheel. We decide not only when to make it stop but also what we want for decisions that we will accept. Learning to control our leadership decision-making process is pivotal to our success. I will share five techniques to help you take control of your focus funnel and ensure it lands on the most helpful leadership decision-making portion of the wheel. But before I do, here's a focus-funnel story to help inspire you to realize you are in control of your focus and, therefore, your direction!

THE WORLD'S GREATEST FAT-BURNING DEVICE

Fifteen years after sitting in the surf zone with Instructor Boston, I formed my small team of five people and raised capital from friends and family to create and market what we all felt was the world's greatest fat-burning device. I had decided that since fitness transformed my life and helped me conquer asthma, I wanted to help other people transform their lives using fitness. To do this meant creating better fitness products that people could enjoy using, because if they enjoyed using our products, then they would see more results. In other words, I wanted to create fitness products that people wanted to use so they could achieve their fitness goals. I found a purpose to my passion of working out and set off with my team to develop a next-generation product that would change the fitness landscape.

By the time I realized that I must create a much simpler product (one that I had sketched years earlier but thought too simple), I was out of money. Still, I was desperate to keep the team together and launch a winning product, so I asked five of my most supportive local investors for a meeting. I was hoping to show them my new product and raise another $100,000, which I figured would get us into initial production.

The meeting was short. I started to introduce the idea of shelving the BodyRev and pursuing a new product. One of the investors said, "Alden, stop. Look at your cash flow statement—you don't have any. We don't want to hear about new products. We are all impressed you persisted as long as you did, but it is time to shut down this business. You only have one option: file for bankruptcy." He let that suggestion hang for a few seconds, before continuing. "You don't have enough money to pay off the lawyers, accountants, and even your manufacturer—it's over. Go bankrupt, get a job, and move on with your life."

I felt like I had been hit by brick, square in the face. I just sat there, one of the rare moments when I was speechless. I eventually muttered something along the lines of "thanks for making the time to meet with me," and then got up and left. I was so shaken by their conviction of what I should do that I just sat in my car.

Bankruptcy was never even in my lexicon. I sat there for a good long while replaying what I had just heard. Each time I replayed their suggestions, I got sick to my stomach. Worse still, my teammates were waiting for me back at the office with great anticipation that I would have been successful raising more capital to keep our dream alive. As I processed what I'd just heard, I also needed to formulate a plan for how to keep the business going.

An hour and a half later (my drive was only twenty minutes—I sat for a good long time thinking), I arrived back at our little office, and one my teammates eagerly asked, "Did you get the funding?"

I didn't immediately respond, and then I looked at them as I slowly said, "I got something better."

They looked at me skeptically, and one of them said, "Ahhh, okay, and that would be?"

"It would be a ninety-day opportunity to prove to our investors that we can build and launch a top-selling product. We have learned so much over the last four years that we have all we need to launch a great product—"

They cut me off. One stated flatly, "He didn't get the money. It's over. We're done."

Another asked, "Alden, how are we going to pay to manufacture the product? We are $500,000 in debt as it is to the manufacturer."

And another stated, "Even if we could get someone to design the product, it takes ninety days to cut steel to make the mold. We don't have enough time, let alone enough money."

All their points were valid concerns. And even though I was expecting them, I didn't have great answers to them. All I had come up with was some logic that I wanted to share. "Look, I hear you all on your points, and I suspect you're right today, but maybe not tomorrow."

Their faces contorted in various dubious expressions as they crossed their arms and looked at me. I reasoned, "I know this much, if we file for bankruptcy, we know exactly what happens—we flush the last four years down the failure drain, and everyone that can help us launch this next product knows that too. They get nothing either if we go bankrupt. What I am proposing is committing for ninety days to launch this product. We have one currency we can use—equity. Let's see if we can convince our vendors with equity to help us bring this product to life, and just for a second imagine with me if this next product works how cool our story will be that we were on the edge of bankruptcy and created an award-winning, kick-ass product."

I let that vision sink in for a moment and then said, "We have enough money to pay everyone's health care for the next ninety days. We'll take it one week at a time and see how far we can get. If after ninety days, or even earlier, we can't make it work, I promise we'll shut down and move on."

I have condensed the conversation a bit, but that was the essence. The team rallied, but it wasn't a week-by-week challenge. It was more like day-by-day, sometimes meeting-by-meeting. For me, I found myself constantly struggling to maintain my can-do focus. There were so many competing and valid reasons why we should not be able to succeed. I knew that if I succumbed to the thought of "we can't do it" that it would quickly infect the others' mindsets. Still, there were plenty of times when I doubted myself, but my team—I think of them as the goal team—lifted me up. No one is a rock all the time.

Eighty-seven days later, the Perfect Pushup launched.

To date, about fifteen million people have bought it (and counting). The Perfect Pushup was one decision away each and every hour during those eighty-seven days from not happening. The difference maker was keeping our focus on taking the next action or figuring out how to make the action occur. The only way we succeeded was through keeping our collective focus on how to make the Perfect Pushup a reality. Fast-forward two and half years, and Perfect Fitness was recognized by *Inc.* magazine as the fastest-growing consumer products company in the United States, with an over 12,000 percent growth rate (we did nearly $100 million in sales in less than three years).

This happened because we kept our focus and kept taking action. It would have been so easy to give up at times as bills stacked up at home and my wife and kids wondered if Dad's idea was going to work. Nights were tough for me. It seemed fear loved to visit me the most when I was alone. On more than one occasion, nightmares of going bankrupt would jolt me from my sleep. I often found myself replaying Instructor Half Butt, Popeye, Boston, Psycho, and Aloha's lessons. They became my nighttime swim buddies to help fend off the repeated attacks from fear's soldiers of doubt, failure, and embarrassment. SEAL Team was the hardest physical test I had done, but launching and growing Perfect Fitness was the hardest civilian test I had encountered, and learning to use the tools from SEAL Team helped my team and me succeed.

Here's the good news: you don't have to go through SEAL training to learn what I am teaching you, but you do need to take the risk of pursuing something new and that still comes with the risk of failure. The fear of failure and the risk that comes with it are the ultimate teacher for learning the techniques I'm sharing.

FIVE FOCUS ACTIONS

Keeping your focus sounds simple, but it's hard work and requires intention. Your focus is yours to own; no one owns your focus but you. There will be moments when you allow your focus to shift to be in alignment with someone else's focus, but remember, you're making that decision. Beware: There are powerful forces at work to grab your focus in order for you to take a desired action, such as "Buy now!" or "Sign up here." Just remember: Your focus is yours to control, and I want you to keep it that way! Here are five techniques I use to keep my focus whether I am climbing a mountain, writing a book, coaching a CEO, or helping my boys achieve something they want but are not sure they can. Surprise! I created an acronym called FOCUS to help you remember these five focus-funnel actions:

- Filter thoughts
- Own outcomes
- Concentrate on the next action
- Understand the why
- Separate what works

What good does it do you if you cannot remember what you are reading? I want you to commit these to memory and practice them daily, for they can change your life—they have changed mine.

Filter Thoughts

As mentioned earlier, we are thought-making machines. We are bombarded with all kinds of thoughts from the past, present, and future every waking moment of our days. Our thoughts are ever present like clouds above our heads (thank you, Byron Katie, for your analogy). Thoughts do not impact us until we attach to them, putting them into our focus funnel. The single, most important first action is deciding which thoughts we want to put into our focus funnel. I call the act of sifting through our thoughts "filtering."

Imagine taking your focus funnel and placing a fine mesh screen over the top of it to prevent "debris"—aka hurtful thoughts—from clogging up your funnel. Think of this screen as an adaptive screen that can open and close on command. If I am surrounded by people sharing all kinds of thoughts that aren't helpful to my efforts to succeed, then I close the screen and let those thoughts float by like clouds rather than focusing on them. I pay no attention to them. See page 170 for an example of a few thoughts that would force me to close my filtering screen.

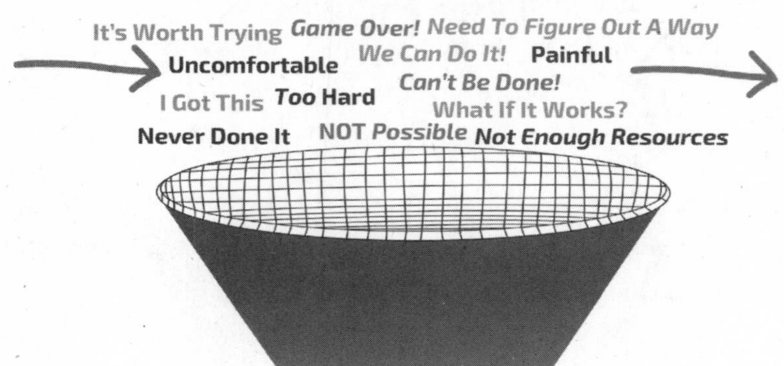

Conversely, when there are thoughts that are helpful to my mission success, I flip an imaginary switch and allow those thoughts to enter my focus funnel. This may seem odd to have your own personal screen to sift through thoughts, but the point is for you to be aware of what you focus on. So often we aren't paying attention to the thoughts we attach to, and before we know it, they grow into beliefs that drive our behaviors into actions that aren't helpful for our long-term success. At that point, we find ourselves wondering why we failed or didn't achieve something while others have. The entire focus (pun intended) of this chapter is to teach you to become aware of your focus and choose the thoughts you want to attach to. Page 171 shows a few examples of thoughts I routinely accept while in pursuit of a goal.

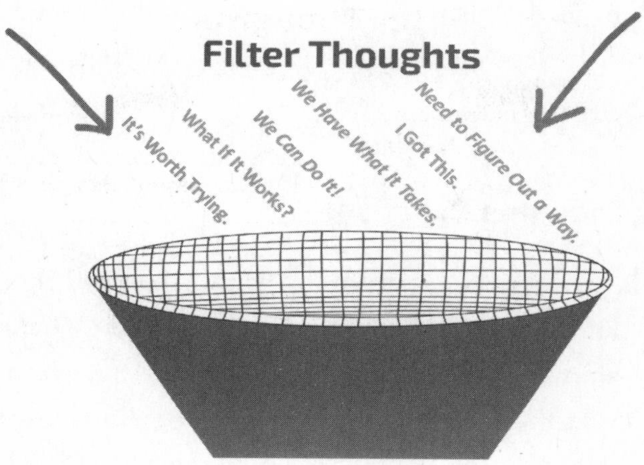

Having a visual representation of the action required to attach to a thought is helpful. Now you need to practice using your own form of an adjustable screen on your focus funnel. Here are two exercises you can use the moment after you read them. Use them throughout your day as you decide to take any kind of action, from doing a chore to working out to deciding which task at work you should work on first.

Our most limited resources are our time, talent, and energy. For us to make the most of our talent we must dedicate time and energy to developing it. The thoughts we focus on directly impact our energy stores. You'll often find this technique helpful when someone you trust bombards you with a series of thoughts that bring into question your resolve or ability to achieve something. In some cases, the five-second rule (see Filter Thoughts Exercises, page 172) can be stretched to the five-hour rule, or more, as you do your own soul searching (research) on whether to accept your trusted advisor's thoughts. Think of this technique as the trust-but-verify approach to accepting a new thought. The five-second rule prompts you to increase your awareness of the thoughts while giving you a grace period in which you can toss them aside or accept them. (Not to worry, if a "hurtful" thought gets by your initial screening, there are other opportunities to remove it from your focus funnel.)

Filter Thoughts Exercises

1. Ask yourself this question: "Is this thought helpful or hurtful to what I am trying to accomplish?" The more you ask yourself this question, the more you will abbreviate it, like I do with my boys, to "helpful or hurtful?" The faster you learn to categorize thoughts, the quicker and more efficient you will be at focusing your energy on those thoughts that will be most helpful to your success.
2. Five-second rule: Give yourself five seconds before you decide to open your focus-funnel screen to ensure that this thought is one worth your energy.

Own Outcomes

I've mentioned several times in this book that *mindsetting* is your greatest leadership challenge. How you lead yourself directly impacts how you lead others. When you ask someone to take charge and make the necessary decision to complete a task, you want them to own that role. The same goes for you when you decide to make a decision on where to put your focus. This can be easier said than done. Your gut (instinct) and heart (feeling) can be telling you, "Go for it!" while your brain (logic) is giving you reasons why you should not move forward. At its simplest, the decision you must own is what to focus on. But how do you make that decision when you have conflicting internal or external voices?

I developed a tool years ago that originated from my rowing and SEAL experiences. I call it an Outcome Account, and it will help you decide where to put your focus. I based the Outcome Account off one of the most challenging classes for me in graduate school: accounting. The simplest form of accounting involves T accounts, a graphical representation of a general ledger that helps categorize credits and debts. I am modifying the T account to capture both future positive and negative outcomes. Here is how it works:

OUTCOME ACCOUNTS: DEFINE YOUR GOAL

+	-
1. Outcomes	1. Outcomes
2. Impact	2. Impact
3. Feel	3. Feel

At the top of the large capital T, write down the goal you seek. Underneath, place a + on the left side and a – on the right side. Start with the positive side and answer these three simple questions:

1. **What is the positive outcome if I achieve this goal?** Envision the positive outcome with all the senses you can muster.
2. **Who is positively impacted if I achieve this goal?** Think about those you care about most that will be positively impacted.
3. **How does this make me feel?** Focus on your feelings. What E-Motions are created from this outcome?

Then perform exactly the same drill but from the negative perspective. So often we enable our focus to be driven solely by our logical brains that we find ourselves out of alignment with what we really want. Using these Outcome Accounts will help surface the best place for your focus.

I use Outcome Accounts all the time, from deciding when to write to starting a workout and committing to a new goal. The simple process helps me fast-forward my decision of where I put my focus, and helps me experience the outcome. Many times I find experiencing the negative outcome can be just as motivating as the positive one. By doing this, you are essentially using your negativity bias as fuel to keep you going. Owning the outcomes of your focus helps keep your focus on what action you need to take next to succeed. Own your outcomes!

Concentrate on the Next Action

We are not good at multitasking—period. The best way to complete an action is to commit and fully focus on the action at hand. Multitasking only slows us down. The energy required to switch between tasks depletes our focus to do one thing well, and instead we end up doing two or more things less than optimally. One of the biggest hole makers for our focus funnel is allowing it to focus on too many things at once. Our focus functions best when we zero in on the one thing we must work on at any given moment, such as climbing a mountain.

To celebrate our fiftieth birthdays, two of my best friends, Brett and Chip, and I decided to climb Denali, the tallest mountain (20,310 feet) in North America. We had climbed several other mountains, but this one would be by far the most challenging one we had ever climbed. One of the aspects that makes climbing Denali so difficult is the climb must be completed without the assistance of additional support climbers. This unsupported climb means that each climber must carry approximately sixty-five pounds on his or her back and tow another sixty-five pounds in a sled in order to haul enough food and gear to survive on the mountain for up to twenty-four days.

Carrying that much weight is hard enough, but carrying and pulling it through snowstorms and steep passes is enough to cause you to seriously question your resolve. I found climbing Denali was as mentally challenging as it was physically. Every day, I broke the climb into fifty-five-minute workout sessions. At the end of each session, our guide would give us a break long enough to eat a couple hundred calories and have a few sips of water, and then the next fifty-five-minute session would begin. Depending on the day, we could do as many as twelve sessions (summit day was the longest). The most mentally exhausting part of the climb is that you never see the summit until forty-five minutes before you make the final turn, just above twenty thousand feet.

For fourteen days, I poured most of my focus into completing one session at a time. During a snowstorm, the pace was so slow that, to keep myself focused, I counted how many steps I took per minute (nineteen) and then repeated the count each minute until break time. When my focus drifted to thoughts wondering, *How much farther to the top?* those were the moments when doubt crept in. The key to climbing *any* mountain—literal or figurative—is focusing on the next step.

When your focus funnel widens too much and you bring in too many thoughts of future work, it can quickly lead you down a path of feeling overwhelmed and losing hope. The only action we can control is the one we take in the present moment. It's important to practice this, and below I share an exercise that helps you do so. I call this the Moment versus the Mountain. I use the word *mountain* to represent the mountain of work ahead of you. Any dream you pursue is going to require mountains of work. I want you to avoid psyching yourself out before you begin your climb toward your dream. Concentrate on the next action you must take—nothing else matters. Use the mountain as a way to track your progress. Charting how far you've come can help you stay positive. But do not dwell on thoughts that are asking you, *How much longer to the top?* Dreams, like mountaintops, are reached one action (one step) at a time.

EXERCISE | The Moment Versus the Mountain

1. **Ask yourself every morning, *What is one action I can take today that will move me closer to achieving my goal?*** You do not climb a big mountain in a day, nor do you achieve a big goal in a single day either. Building the habit of taking daily action toward your goal is a critical habit for an Unstoppable Mindset.

2. **Calendar your one action per day.** When you put your actions in your calendar, you will find it easier to build your daily habit of taking action. I write mine down on a three-by-five index card. I even created my own daily action cards (see www.BeUnstoppable.com/DailyActionCards for more information). I find it helpful to schedule my daily action earlier in the day. If not, the rest of the day's unexpected activities seem to always get in the way.

Understand the Why

In the goal-setting section of this book, I asked you not only to define *what* you want but also *why* you want it. This is an important two-step process. The *what* typically appeals to the logical portion of your brain: "I want a promotion to VP," "I want to make the varsity team," or "I want to build my own business." Defining a measurable *what* is a very important first step—it gives our brain direction.

Defining the *why* gives us fuel to fend off fear. When it looks like nothing is going our way and we begin to question our resolve to continue working toward our dream, we will find energy to persist from our *why*. A proper *why* blends two powerful energy sources together: passion and purpose. Remember to think of these two powers as two oars in a rowboat. When you row with both oars, you go forward. If you have only one, you will find yourself going in circles. From my experience, it doesn't matter which portion of the *why* you start with. What matters most is that you find passion in your purpose or purpose in your passion. You need both as fuel for pressing on when the going gets tough.

The second time I looked at bankruptcy was right after we received the *Inc. 500* award. Not only had we been recognized as one of the fastest-growing companies, but we also received a $150 million offer to buy our company. As we pursued the sale of the company, the worst financial crisis of the twenty-first century occurred. During the swearing-in process for President Obama, he declared this was the second Great Depression of the United States. Within weeks, the offer to buy the company was rescinded, and the bank we used to grow our business froze our assets and demanded we pay them what we owed in less than thirty days. (We were $8.8 million in debt to the bank, and we had used our houses as collateral.)

Once again, I found myself staring squarely at bankruptcy, except this time it was not investors informing me of my only option. It was lawyers, bankers, and accountants. I had felt like I had gone from hero to zero in less than thirty days. Literally at the beginning of the week, I was in New York City appearing on network television shows, and by the end of the week, I was discussing how to save my house while shutting down the business.

During one of those sleepless nights, I drove down to the office on a Sunday evening, grabbed the mail from the weekend, and sat looking at the products we had developed. I just couldn't believe I was grappling with going bankrupt—again. As I flipped through the mail, one envelope stood out: a letter addressed to "Mr. Perfect Pushup Man," written in pencil. It read:

Dear Mr. Perfect Pushup Man,

My grandmother gave me the Perfect Pushup. She bought it at Walmart. I followed your workout four times [each workout routine is three weeks—he did twelve weeks of push-ups], *and I am proud to tell you I made the JV football team. Next year I am trying out for varsity. Thank you for inventing the Perfect Pushup.*

Johnny #25

There was my *why* written in gray number two pencil on white, wide-lined paper. Reading that letter reconnected my focus with why I started the company in the first place. I had grown apart from my *why* over the last couple of years. My focus had shifted to feeding the retail machines of Walmart, Dick's, Target, Costco, Carrefour, Tesco, and so many others around the world. I had forgotten why I wanted to be in the business in the first place. That night and in large part thanks to Johnny, I made the decision we would not file for bankruptcy, and we would not accept a discount on paying back our loan. We would pay it back in full; we just needed three hundred days instead of thirty. And like every other accomplishment in life, I had a swim buddy (Andrew Morrison) help make this goal a reality. It was a tremendous team effort and one that I am proud to say we achieved (paid our loan back in full) in 293 days in large part by using the Moment versus the Mountain exercise every day!

No matter what dream you seek, learn to connect your passion and purpose for that dream. If you cannot find both, then hit the pause button until you do know them both. Every challenging dream I have ever accomplished required me to access the energy of my *why*. When everything else is going to hell in a handbasket, your *why* will give you the power to persist.

EXERCISE | **Understanding Your Why**

1. The energy source of your *why* is E-Motion. One of my favorite President Lincoln quotations is, "To win a person to your cause, you must first reach their heart, the great high road to their reason." Understanding your *why* means connecting with your heart and tapping into the E-Motions that drive you.
2. Ask yourself, *Why am I passionate about this dream?* and *What is the purpose of my dream* (aka who does it help beside yourself and how does it make you feel when you help them)*?*

Separate What Works

The definition of insanity I most relate to is "doing the same thing again and again while expecting a different result." In SEAL Team, you can learn very quickly and sometimes painfully what doesn't work. Hopefully, you don't learn those lessons through injury and death, but sadly, there are times that it happens. Training for SEAL missions is the ultimate culling process of detaching your emotion from ideas to get to the idea that works best. We often said, "The ego is not our amigo." Someone who gets hell-bent focused on their idea can lose focus on better ideas, which might get someone injured or gear damaged.

There are countless stories in SEAL Teams where platoons did not focus on separating what worked from what didn't, and the end results were catastrophic. When the mission starts, we often say, that's when the mission plan ends. You must be able to keep your focus on what works. If your focus remains attached to a plan because "it's your idea" or you have some emotional connection to one idea over another, you can find yourself in trouble quickly. The key to flexibility is not being attached to the idea but instead attaching to the ideas that help you move forward the best.

This shift in focus can be challenging, especially if you are the one in charge. When the title associated with your name conveys that you are the senior leader, you can instinctively feel like you must come up with the best ideas. When you are leading yourself toward your goal, the same phenomenon occurs. Our egos get in the way and tell us we don't need to listen to anyone else. Sometimes this might work, but most of the time, what's required is a shift in our focus from *who* to *how*. Don't focus on *whose* idea it is. Focus on *how* well the idea works. The ultimate arbiter of ideas is what works best.

I spent four years putting good money after bad trying to launch a product that people were just not buying. I finally switched my focus with the help of my single most important investor who happened to also moonlight as my executive coach, main cheerleader, and held the full-time role as my father-in-law, aka "Pops." I was literally so broke that when Pops and my mother-in-law asked us to come visit them in the San Juan Islands, I needed to ask them for help buying airplane tickets.

The first night we arrived was a beautiful evening. In summers on the San Juans, the sunsets last for hours and with stunning golden-orange afterglows. Before dinner, we all sat on the porch watching the sun set over Canada. Pops asked me how the business was going.

I responded as cheerfully as I could, saying, "We have figured out a new approach, Pops. I'm really excited about it."

He looked at me questioningly while raising one eyebrow. "Oh really, and what might that approach be?"

I took a deep breath and said enthusiastically, "We're shifting our focus to build a new product."

He did not blink as he stared directly at me and said in a command voice, “Pooh [his affectionate term for me—it’s a longer story—his son was my Navy SEAL swim buddy], join me on the point for a moment.”

We walked just out of earshot of my mother-in-law and wife as he put his arm around my shoulder (he’s a big man at nearly six five, a former University of Washington Rose Bowl football player) and said, “Keep looking straight ahead. Can you hear me?”

As I locked my stare on the horizon, I said sheepishly, “Ahh, sure can, Pops.”

“Good, because I want you to hear me very clearly. I didn’t raise my daughter to marry a f^%*$ng aerobics instructor. I will give you six months to figure out your next product. Then you are getting a job.” He paused for a moment. “Did you hear that?”

I slowly nodded my head and said, “Yep, sure did, Pops.”

He then smacked me on the back, smiled at me, and said, “Good talk. Let’s go get some dinner!”

Over dinner, my mother-in-law, who is an amazing cook, kept commenting, “Alden, what’s wrong with you? You usually eat so much more. Here, let me serve you some more food.”

I had lost my appetite for food while focusing on trying to figure out how we could possibly launch a new product in six months. Pops’s lifeline of support came with a six-month timeline that dramatically narrowed my focus. Before, I had not put hard-and-fast timelines on milestones in the business; they were more like suggestions. Now I was faced with figuring out how to launch an entirely new product in three months and then get three months of sales to prove that this new product could work. I had no interest in eating. My sole focus was how we could build and launch a product in three months.

As simple as it sounds, focusing on separating what works from what doesn't is no easy task when you're attached emotionally to ideas that you created or when someone you care about influences your focus. Remember the focus-funnel rules—your funnel is agnostic, and it acts like a magnet. That can work for or against you if you aren't careful. Building a separating habit between things that work and throwing out the things that don't will allow you to move forward more quickly.

In much the same way that champions have selective memories, that is the point of separating what works: distinguishing those memories/thoughts that can help you succeed from those that hold you back. Other than what you can learn from your failure, it does you no good keeping your focus on it. Learning to let go of what doesn't work and keeping your focus on what does or could work is another essential feature of an Unstoppable Mindset.

EXERCISE | **Separate What Works**

When you are in the thick of it trying to figure out what is working best for you, it is often most helpful to find different perspectives. The term *triangulation* is used for finding your location when conducting land navigation. You take three compass readings from known landmarks to give you a triangulated position of approximately where you are. You can use the same technique for helping you keep your focus on what works. Instead of landmarks, find three goal team members who you trust to give you honest feedback. Identify three people (whether you make them part of your goal team or not is up to you) whose advice you can seek about keeping your focus on what is most important to your success.

FOCUS SUMMARY

Learning to control our focus is a critical action of building an Unstoppable Mindset. Our focus funnel is agnostic: it doesn't care if we put helpful or hurtful thoughts in it. Moreover, our focus acts as a magnet and will attract like energy. Focus on negativity and you will get more of it. Conversely, focus on positivity and you will find more positivity. There are five essential focus techniques detailed in this chapter, which are captured by the acronym **FOCUS**.

Filter thoughts—thoughts are ever present and are neither helpful nor hurtful until we attach to them. Think of putting a screen over your focus funnel that allows you to control which thoughts you focus on.

Own outcomes—many times our focus can drift to future negative thoughts that create anxiety. To prevent anxiety or negative thoughts from derailing our focus on achieving a goal, use an Outcome Account to outline both positive and negative outcomes. Outcome Accounts enable you to envision (experience) the future outcome both positively and negatively. The emotions created will provide you fuel to persist.

Concentrate on the next action—we have three kinds of thoughts: past, present, and future. The thought that matters most is the one we can act on in this moment. All too often we will allow our focus to drift to the mountain of future work in front of us, which can cause us to build negative hypotheticals. To avoid becoming overwhelmed by all the work yet to be accomplished, ask yourself, *What can I do right now?* Nothing else matters but the action you take in the moment.

Understand the *why*—our focus remains strong when we know our *whys*, and a *why* has two key sources of energy: passion and purpose. It doesn't matter which one comes first. Instead, what matters most is linking these together, which will provide the resolve you need to press on in trying times. Understand your *why* and you will always be able to focus on figuring out your way forward.

Separate what works—one of the quickest ways to lose your focus is from failure. Learn to use failure as fuel by seeing it as a learning opportunity. Don't attach your focus to the failures. Separate what works from what doesn't and move on. Champions have selective memories. Keep your focus on finding the actions that will help you move forward, and disregard the rest.

Beliefs
8

BELIEVE TO ACHIEVE

The reason beliefs are so important is because we associate truth with them. I discuss beliefs last because it typically takes thoughts and focus to make a belief. I say typically because there are times when we blindly accept a belief from someone we trust, for example, a close friend, an expert (e.g., a doctor, lawyer, or consultant), or a family member. Even then, we take a thought, focus on it, and attach truth to that thought. When we decide that a particular thought is true and then look for ways to reinforce it, we are elevating that thought's status to a belief. A belief is "an acceptance that a statement is true or that something exists." What gives a belief meaning is the attachment to truth. A belief is a thought that is true to us.

The Naval Academy football team had a long-standing belief that it could not beat Notre Dame. It was the longest consecutive losing streak in Division I FBS football history at forty-three years. The Navy Midshipmen had good reasons to believe they couldn't beat Notre Dame. For starters, all service academies have height and weight restrictions, students cannot red-shirt (they must graduate in four years), and must serve in the Navy for five years upon graduation (i.e., NFL opportunities are essentially nonexistent). Furthermore, the last time Navy beat Notre Dame was in 1963, with Heisman Trophy winner Roger Staubach. The Middies had lots of good reasons to support their long-held belief that Navy would never beat Notre Dame.

However, in 2001, a new coach, Paul Johnson, came to Annapolis. His first order of business was to shift the Navy players' mindsets. In the team locker room on a large dry-erase board, he wrote and reminded them daily: "Believe to Achieve." He got them to shift their focus from what they didn't have to what they could do, and year after year, challenged their limiting beliefs of why they couldn't beat Notre Dame to a new empowering belief that they could. In 2007, during a triple-overtime thriller, Navy beat Notre Dame for the first time in forty-four years, and they did it without a Heisman winner (they didn't even have a Heisman hopeful on the team).

Coach Johnson left to coach Georgia Tech a year later and left the Navy football reins to his assistant Ken Niumatalolo. His protégé coach kept the belief alive and went on to beat Notre Dame three more times.

When you compare the two teams from size to skill levels on paper, it's a lopsided comparison that overwhelmingly favors Notre Dame. Players can be there up to six years, there are no height and weight standards, and many top high school players are attracted to the school because of its history of NFL recruitment. It is truly a David-versus-Goliath story. Navy's success did not happen overnight. One simple slogan of "Believe to Achieve" didn't lead them to victory by chance. It did, however, help to shift their focus to change their beliefs. Coach Johnson went to work on them believing each and every day in themselves. In the locker room and on the practice field is where he wanted them to believe first. To achieve anything, the first step is in believing you can achieve it.

But it can be very difficult to believe in something that others vehemently believe isn't possible. For instance, imagine every well-known expert from doctor to coach, competitor, and critic believing that running a sub-four-minute mile was "humanly impossible." They would offer all kinds of statistics that spanned from the physical limits of the human body to the impracticality of achieving the feat. Their beliefs in what they knew to be true were reasonable and clearly accepted by a large majority of people, except one competitor named Roger Bannister. He was not your typical professional athlete. He practiced away from the noise of those who said it couldn't be done. Critics and coaches referred to him as a lone wolf, as he did not follow traditional training regimes. His main focus was practicing as a junior doctor. His training was limited, and he used pacing teammates to help him maintain the winning pace he was seeking.

On May 6, 1954, Roger Bannister became the first human to break the four-minute mile at a time of 3:59.4 seconds. Here's the most fascinating portion of the story: his record only lasted forty-six days, after which an Australian, John Landry, smashed it by over a second. The following year, three more people broke the record that athletes and coaches had been trying to break since 1886. Today more than 1,700 people have broken what was long considered unachievable.

What was the difference maker in helping Roger break through a long considered insurmountable barrier? I suspect you can guess by now: he believed he could do it. That belief drove him to try different training techniques. He was willing to experiment. When he came in fourth at the Helsinki Olympics, he viewed his results in the 1,500-meter as a positive, and it strengthened his resolve to keep trying. In much the same way the Midshipmen of the Naval Academy learned to believe in their abilities one practice at a time, Roger Bannister did too, quite literally one running stride at a time.

An empowering belief that helps you to do something you have never done before is not built overnight. Instead, it's built through actions that remind and reinforce your resolve in accepting a belief that you can do it. In this chapter, I will share a multistep process called I-CAN (identify, challenge, assess, and neutralize) as a framework for building empowering beliefs. This structure is designed to remind and reinforce your resolve to believe you can do something you have never done before.

BELIEFS 101

Before we dive into how to change a limiting belief into an empowering one, let's discuss what I call Beliefs 101: what they are, where they come from, and why they are so powerful. As mentioned earlier, beliefs are nothing more than thoughts we have accepted as the truth. This attachment process of connecting the truth with a thought in itself is not helpful or hurtful. It only becomes impactful to us when we decide to take a corresponding action based on the belief. The reason beliefs are so powerful is they act like a seed. If you imagine for a moment that your brain is nothing more than soil and the seeds you plant in it are thoughts, the only way to grow those seeds into fruitful plants is through fertilizing them.

In my analogy, the brain is the soil, the thought is a seed, and the fertilizer is our focused energy on attaching to that thought. The more we focus on it, the more it gets fertilized, and the process of attaching or fertilizing a thought makes the seed sprout into a belief. When the belief grows, so do the actions we take to support the belief. In the beginning, we may only take intentional actions because we are still becoming accustomed to this new plant we are tending to. These initial actions are called behaviors, and they originate from the seed of our thoughts.

For example, I was told (more like teased) I had big legs and couldn't jump, and therefore I'd be a terrible basketball player. I knew my legs were larger than most kids on my team, and I accepted that. But what I had not thought about until several kids kept reminding me (teasing publicly) was that because of my "thunder thighs," I couldn't move as fast or jump as high as needed to be a good basketball player. At first, I didn't believe my legs were the problem, but after a few bad passes, rebounds, and shots I started accepting what they were saying was true. And the more I did that, the more I played poorly. My teammates' belief in me became my own because I decided to accept their opinion of why I wouldn't be a good basketball player. In essence, their belief became my self-fulfilling prophecy because I attached to it (fertilized it) and began behaving in accordance with the belief that I wasn't a good basketball player.

Going back to my seed analogy, soil doesn't care what you grow in it (I know there are limits, but I'm speaking in general terms). You can plant petunias, potatoes, or poison oak. The difference maker is the seed (thought) you decide to fertilize. The more nutrients (energy) you give the seed, the more the seed takes shape into something that requires you to take action (pruning, trimming, etc.). Seeds are just seeds until you give them energy to grow. The same goes for thoughts.

If your initial thought is, *I can't do this*, and you keep giving that thought-focused energy, you will find yourself taking actions that support that thought. When this happens, you have formed a belief and have created behaviors (actions) in alignment with your belief. This process of belief-to-behavior becomes even more important over time, because if the behaviors are reinforced/practiced enough times they become habit forming. Once they have developed into a habit, it becomes even more difficult for you to be aware of the actions you are taking because habits are essentially actions you take automatically.

INSTRUCTOR ALOHA

BUD/S comprises three phases of training creatively called first phase, second phase, and third phase. Each phase comes with big challenges. In first phase, Hell Week is the major challenge and is responsible for the greatest number of dropouts in SEAL Training. In second phase, the toughest obstacle is called pool competency (aka pool comp), a week-long series of intense SCUBA diving tests in an Olympic-size pool called the combat training tank. It is the source of the largest number of failures (drops from training), and it was one of the challenges I was actually looking forward to.

I was that kid who wore my mask and fins to watch *Flipper*, the 1960s television show that featured a Florida Keys park ranger, his two boys, and their pet dolphin, Flipper. From a young age, I lived for playing in, on, or under the water. When I turned twelve, I convinced my dad to take SCUBA diving lessons with me (I needed a parent with me in order to take the class). By the end of that summer, I was diving every chance I got. I loved the feeling of being underwater and spent the next ten years diving all around New England. I figured, if I could make it through Hell Week, then I would definitely make it through pool comp. After all, I had ten years of diving experience.

Pool comp lived up to the hype as the toughest challenge in second phase. Each day seemed harder than the last, with a stressful underwater final exam on Friday morning. Since I was one of the class leaders, I was required to go first while the rest of the class was ordered to sit facing away from the pool so they couldn't see what was happening. The final pool comp test lasted about twenty minutes. Two SEAL instructors were assigned to each student, and they took turns "attacking," or presenting the test taker with different underwater problems.

You were wearing a pair of SCUBA tanks connected to an unusual regulator system (air hoses) not found in the civilian diving market—I had never used this system before. The instructors hovered above the student and took turns diving down creating challenges such as removing your mask, tossing and turning you, and various knot-tying tricks with your breathing hose. Through each obstacle they created, the student was expected to follow a very specific series of protocols. If at any time they didn't like what they saw, they would tap you three times on your head to signify the command "come to the surface—training is over."

I started the test on my hands and knees in the nine-foot section of the pool, slowly crawling on all fours from one side of the pool to the next. During my first "attack," my regulator was ripped from my mouth, and my mask was taken away. Before I could get my breathing hose, the second instructor wrapped me up in a wrestling move, tossing and rolling me several times. I could not reach my mouthpiece because it was stuck behind my head. As I started to initiate the standard operating procedure for removing my tanks, I received three taps on the head. I had been underwater for about ninety seconds.

Once on the surface, one of my attackers said, "Mr. Mills, you failed. Get out of the pool and face the wall." I couldn't believe what I was hearing. The one activity in all of SEAL training that I thought I would be great at, I had just failed within less than two minutes.

As I walked over to the wall, I could hear my classmates mumbling, "Sir, what happened?" "Do you know why you failed?" "I can't believe Mr. Mills failed."

I sat there staring at the light-brown bricks for three hours pondering what had gone wrong. For the life of me, I could not figure it out.

That afternoon I had another attempt at the pool comp test. I lasted three minutes. I wasn't alone—nearly half the class had failed (about ten people).

The lead instructor of the pool comp test said, "Gentlemen, you have one more opportunity to pass this test. If you do not pass on Monday morning, you'll be officially dropped from BUD/S. You are to report to the parking lot of second phase tomorrow morning [Saturday] at 0700 hours to meet Instructor Aloha for remedial training. Good luck."

Instructor Aloha was from the North Shore of Oahu and was a well-known big-wave surfer before he joined the Navy and became a SEAL. Imagine a Hawaiian lifeguard who stood about five ten, weighed about 185 pounds, and had a permanent smile on his face. He spoke with a thick Hawaiian accent and always greeted us with a big "Aloooo*ha*, Class 181!" He might have had the outward appearance of a happy Hawaiian, but he could deliver big waves full of pain while never losing his smile, which made him someone to be feared. And he didn't disappoint that weekend.

One of the biggest challenges of the pool comp test was staying calm while running out of air. The procedures you must follow to remove your tanks are very specific and unique to BUD/S. It's not complicated when you practice them while not worrying about breathing, but they become a lot more difficult to execute when you are holding your breath for so long that your throat starts making noises like a dolphin as you fight your body's natural urge to breathe. The irony of my two failures was that I didn't even feel like I had gotten to the point where I was running out of air before I was told to resurface. Both of my head taps came early into my breath holds, and I kept replaying what I had done but couldn't understand why I'd failed until I met with Instructor Aloha the next morning.

We were all standing at attention in the second phase parking lot at five minutes before 7:00 a.m. (standard arrival time before any exercise in BUD/S). The parking area was surrounded by a tall, shrouded fence to prevent outsiders from looking in. At exactly 7:00 a.m., Instructor Aloha arrived wearing a pair of old flip-flops and a wide-brimmed straw lifeguard hat, holding a clipboard in his hand as he smiled broadly and said, "Aloooo*ha*, Class 181!"

We responded with our customary, "Hooyah, Instuctor Aloha!"

He grinned as his eyes scanned all of ours, and then he stated, "My tadpoles, you ain't gonna earn yah frog legs if yah don't pass this final test on Monday. Today I'm gonna teach yah how to pass it, and to do it means I have to introduce yah to the Big Kahuna in the sky."

It is never a good sign when a Navy SEAL instructor tells you he is going to introduce you to God at the start of a training exercise. Instructor Aloha made good on his promise. Before we started, he read from the clipboard the reasons why each of us failed. We had failed because we didn't follow the standard operating procedures (SOPs) that the dive instructors had taught us earlier in the week. When he read out my failure, he said, "Mr. Mills, yah learn to dive before coming here, haven't yah?"

I nodded.

"Hmmm, I'm gonna need to break ah bad civilian habit—no dropping the weight belt first; it's the last thing that leaves your body." Then it hit me. I hadn't even realized it, but I was dropping my weight belt before doing any other procedure, which is the complete opposite of what they teach in BUD/S. For ten years, I had believed and practiced that the very first thing to do was drop your weight belt.

Over the next several hours, Instructor Aloha had us perform a series of simple tasks while holding our breath. He would "hide" a mask, fin, and snorkel in plain sight in twenty-five-yard intervals throughout the parking lot. He labeled each one with a number, for example Mask—1, Fin—2, and Snorkel—3. He would then make a starting line that also doubled as a finish line, time us for one minute while we held our breath, and then call out a three-digit combination such as three, one, two. At which point, we would collect the three objects in the order he called out and then return to where we started while holding our breath the entire time.

The first few times were relatively easy, but then he added a fourth object, a weight belt, and then a fifth, a helmet. By the time we were retrieving five objects, we started passing out before we completed his exercise. By the end of day, every one of us had bloodied knees, elbows, and chins from blacking out while collecting all of the objects. Though I may not have seen God, I definitely saw stars!

The next day, Instructor Aloha had us wearing twin SCUBA tanks (the same ones used during pool comp) and a weight belt. This time we sat on the ground as we did exactly the same breath-hold timing drills, except this time he assigned numbers to the five straps (and weight belt) and called out the specific order that we needed to follow to pass the pool comp test. The weight belt was number five—it was always the last in the sequence in SEAL Team.

I spent that evening in my room practicing the sequence on an imaginary set of tanks while holding my breath. Little did I realize, Instructor Aloha's simple but effective technique for simulating the underwater stress of running out of air while focusing on the SOPs helped me quickly form a new habit that aided me in passing pool comp on Monday morning.

The power of beliefs played a crucial role in my ability to overcome the challenges of pool comp. As an experienced diver, I had developed certain beliefs about how to handle underwater situations that were deeply ingrained in my mind. These beliefs, formed through years of civilian diving experience, were now working against me in the high-stakes environment of SEAL training. The realization that my previously held beliefs were hindering my progress was a humbling and eye-opening experience. It was only by acknowledging and confronting these beliefs that I was able to adapt and ultimately succeed.

Instructor Aloha's remedial training not only taught us the correct techniques for passing pool comp but also instilled in us the importance of questioning our beliefs and being open to change. Through this process, we discovered the power of embracing new beliefs that aligned with our goals as SEAL candidates. As we shed our old habits and adopted a new mindset, we found ourselves better equipped to face the challenges that lay ahead.

This transformative experience serves as a powerful reminder that our beliefs can either propel us forward or hold us back. By examining and challenging our beliefs, we can unlock our true potential and achieve success in all aspects of life. Whether in the unforgiving world of SEAL training or the everyday challenges we face, the power of beliefs is undeniable, and harnessing that power can lead to extraordinary results.

BELIEF > BEHAVIORS > HABITS

The reason beliefs are so powerful is that they drive us to take corresponding actions. Initially, these actions are behaviors, which are actions that we take intentionally. When we decide to do something for the first time, we focus very specifically on the actions required to complete the task. From shooting a basketball to removing SCUBA tanks underwater, we must think about the order of the actions needed to perform the function. If we practice these sets of actions long enough, they become second nature to us as if we are performing them automatically. When the actions become automatic, we have formed a habit. When this happens, our brain is essentially on autopilot, freeing up more of our consciousness to focus on other, more intentional actions.

I really like the way Charles Duhigg, author of *The Power of Habit*, describes a habit: "A habit is like a sequence of code that contains a series of actions." I think of a habit like a line of computer code (not that I am any good at writing computer code) that, when run, a series of actions happens, such as "dropping the weight belt" or "shooting a basketball."

The key to a habit is ensuring you are taking the correct actions for the outcome you seek. In the case of shooting a basketball, my "code" was programmed with an initial command (belief) that said, *You won't make the basket because you are bad at basketball.* This line of code started a series of subsequent actions that ensured I would miss the shot. In the case of the pool comp test, my habit code started with the command (belief), *If no air, drop weight belt first.* In computer lingo, the belief is the initial command, and the codes (actions) that follow are built upon the command. Here's how I think about it:

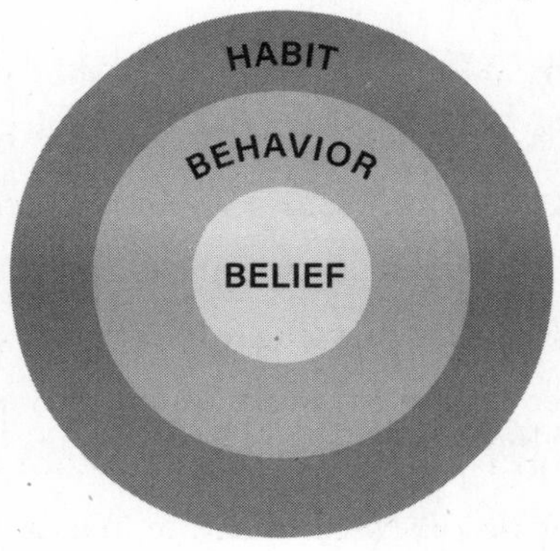

The belief sets the command for the type of actions required. If your belief command is "you cannot beat Notre Dame," then your thoughts and focus will align with your belief and you will take a series of actions that support your belief—in this case, to not beat Notre Dame. Beliefs begin a snowball effect of actions that will help you achieve whatever you believe you can achieve. Over time, you will build habits to support your beliefs. Along the way, some habits will not be helpful to you in your journey to achieve your dream. This is normal and to be expected. Remember: We are human, which means we are imperfect! There's a saying Marshall Goldsmith writes about: "What got you here won't get you there." This applies not only to climbing a corporate ladder but also when trying to achieve something new to you.

In other words, part of building an Unstoppable Mindset has to do with screening your beliefs, behaviors, and habits that might be limiting your success. Sometimes you will find them by discovering a habit that no longer serves you like I did in BUD/S when I realized the civilian habit of dropping my weight belt first was no longer helpful. Those are the simple habits to correct. The more challenging habits are the ones that require you to change your belief from "I can't" to "I can."

Pick the analogy you like—seed or computer code—your belief is what starts the action process. Achieving anything first begins with believing. Nothing is ever achieved until you first believe you can do it. So how do you switch your belief from "I can't" to "I can"? Use the four actions in the I-CAN process.

I-CAN

The essence of all leadership comes down to deciding whether you can or cannot do something. Which is why I created an acronym called I-CAN to capture the four actions required to change a belief. Remember: My use of acronyms is creating something that captures the goal of what I want you to remember. One of the key takeaways I want you to remember from this book is: *you decide what you can or cannot do.* No one else decides but you. What you lead yourself to do or not to do is up to you. Your beliefs play a critical role in what you decide you can or cannot achieve. There will be plenty of times throughout your life where you will be forced to change a belief to accomplish what you desire.

I changed my belief that, because I was born with smaller-than-average-size lungs and asthma, I had to lead a less-active lifestyle; or that as a sophomore I could not make the varsity rowing team; or that I could not graduate from the Naval Academy; or that I needed asthma medicine in SEAL training; or that we did not have enough money or time to build the Perfect Pushup; or that I could not be an author because I got bad grades in English class. These are just a few of the beliefs that I have tackled over the past forty years, and I changed them by following these four actions: identify, challenge, assess, and neutralize (I-CAN). These are the steps to changing a belief.

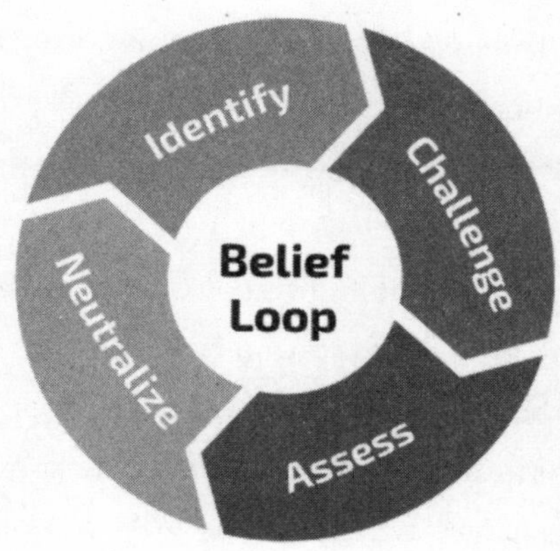

Identify

The first action to change a belief is learning what you want to change. It may seem easy, but when it comes to your beliefs that you have accepted, it can be really hard to discover the belief that is holding you back. There is this old saying, "Fish discovered water last." Finding your limiting belief can feel like being a fish that is discovering water for the first time. There are two techniques I have found most beneficial to uncovering a belief that is no longer helpful on my journey to achieve my goal: the five whys and triangulation.

Five Whys

In the 1970s, Toyota wanted to improve the quality of their cars. With the help of some industrial consultants, they created a simple system for finding the root cause of a quality problem. They found that on average it took five questions asking "why?" to get to the reason behind the problem. Here is an example:

1. Why did the car fail inspection?
   Answer: It had only four lug nuts on the right front wheel.
2. Why did the right front wheel have only four lug nuts on it?
   Answer: The assembler at station twenty-two received only four lug nuts.
3. Why did the assembler at station twenty-two receive only four lug nuts?
   Answer: One of the lug nuts bounced out on the conveyor belt before arriving to station twenty-two.
4. Why did the lug nut bounce out?
   Answer: The conveyor belt track has some broken (worn) wheels on it.

5. Why isn't the conveyor belt track fixed?
   Answer: Because we don't routinely check the track.

By using the five whys line of questioning, one answer leads to another that eventually leads to the real issue. Uncovering the root cause is like peeling back the proverbial layers of the onion to get to the heart of it. In the example, the core problem is that the conveyor belt track is not routinely checked. The same general idea can work for you when trying to identify the belief that is holding you back from achieving the success you seek. Here is an example that I used to tell myself for years when it came to writing a book:

1. Why don't you write a book?
   Answer: I am not a writer.
2. Why don't you think you are a writer?
   Answer: Because I'm not good at writing.
3. Why do you think you are not good at writing?
   Answer: Because I did not get good grades in English class in high school.
4. Why do you think you did not get good grades in English class?
   Answer: Because I always messed up using run-on sentences and sentence fragments.
5. Why were you not any good with sentence structure?
   Answer: Because I was bored in class.

This is one of the beliefs I had before I started committing myself to writing. I literally had to overcome an old belief that, because I stunk at sentence composition (in particular run-on sentences), I couldn't write a book. Once I figured out that the limiting belief keeping me from my goal of writing a book came down to something I'd accepted as true twenty years earlier, I then used triangulation to help me identify a new belief that would help me achieve my goal.

Triangulation

The technique for using a compass to discover your position on a map is called triangulation, and I use it as an analogy for helping me accept a new belief (and I also referenced this tool in the prior chapter regarding the fifth action of FOCUS: Separate what works). To find your position on a map using a compass, you must take bearings to three known points. For instance, known points could be a mountaintop, a bend in a river, and a large rock formation.

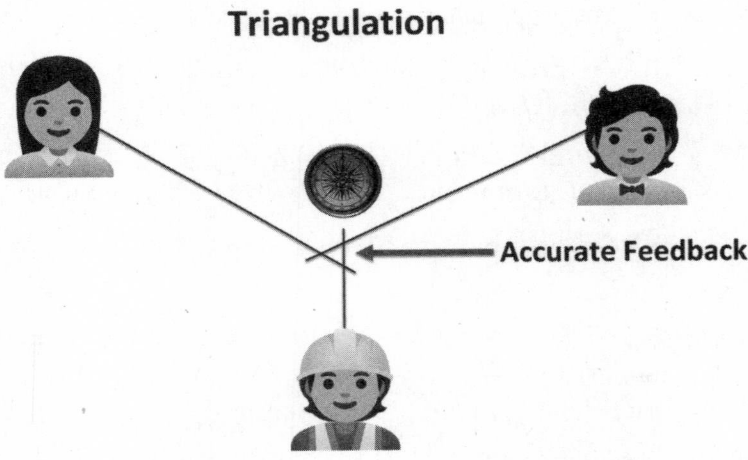

The intersection of these three points creates a triangle, and that triangle represents your location. The same works when you are deciding on a new belief. Find three trusted people who know something about the goal you're trying to achieve. In my case, the first trusted person I found was an expert in communications. He gave me a book that helped me debunk the idea that I couldn't write (it also confirmed that I was not alone regarding being bored in English class). The second was my father-in-law, who had written a book in his spare time and told me how he did it (and reassured me that he never thought of himself as a writer either). The third was a classmate from high school who was now a publisher and explained what editors do (and again, encouraged me that I too could write a book).

It took three totally different people to finally get me to embrace the belief that I could write a book, and even then, I had plenty of times when I would seek encouragement from them. These people represented my goal team for writing a book. (Today, my goal team for writing a book has many more "goal buds"!) To help you identify the new belief, you must adopt a new empowering one. Start by finding three different people who have accomplished the goal you seek. When you speak with them, ask them about their beliefs around how they did what they did or do, and what you will find is a belief that will be helpful to you in your journey to success.

Ask your trusted teammates: "What do you tell yourself when you are taking X action?"

Challenge

We know that behind any limiting belief is fear. Fear is our constant foe in life. It can fuel us to move forward or stop us in our tracks. Fear can be so overwhelming at times that we'll be scared enough to stop before we even try. Fear is always with us, and the best way to deal with it is to embrace it. There are two basic fears: the fear of staying put and the fear of moving forward. Until the fear of staying put is *greater* than the fear of moving forward, we will stay put. When we decide to achieve something, we must deal with these two fears.

When we are younger, we have a greater tolerance for risk and the associated fear that comes with it. As we get older and accept more responsibility, we become more calculating in the amount of risk we wish to accept. I'm not here to tell you how much risk you should face. However, I do want to make you aware of how fear can alter your direction in life. The point of the challenge phase of changing a belief is confronting the fear that is associated with the belief you seek to change.

Ultimately, the decision is yours on whether to change the belief that will alter your direction. However, for you to make an informed decision means you must challenge the original premise for the existing belief. What we accepted as true at one point in our lives may no longer be valid to us, but until we identify and then challenge it, we will find ourselves anchored to our original belief.

Remember from chapter five what fear does to our brain—it activates the amygdala, which can put us in fight, flight, or freeze mode. If we aren't careful, we'll make decisions based on fear rather than on facts that can help us succeed. When challenging an existing belief, use an Outcome Account to project a moment in the future if you decide not to take action and stay put. Ask yourself how this decision to stay put will feel in the future. What will your life be like? Activate as many senses as you can. Is this the life you want in the future? Who is impacted by your belief to stay put, and how does this make you feel? As you answer these questions, you'll begin to envision a future state of what your life is like when you keep deciding to stay put.

Now, do exactly the same drill except with the outcome of you deciding to move forward in going after your dream. What is your life like? Is this the life you want in the future? Who is impacted by it and how does this make you feel? Play these outcome scenarios in your head as many as times as you like. The more you play them, the more you will decide which belief is the one you wish to accept. By envisioning a vivid outcome movie of what happens when you stay put, you may very well realize that your original belief of why you cannot do something isn't that terrifying once you see how that belief holds you back from the life you want.

Identifying the limiting belief is helpful. Understanding its long-term impact can be life changing. As scared as you might be about trying to move forward on something you have never done before, realizing what your life is like by never trying and staying put can be all the fuel you need to take action toward your dream! Remember: The challenge here is confronting the fear that holds you back versus the fear of moving forward. When you understand the longer-term consequences of staying put, you may decide that it's worth the risk of facing the fear of moving forward. In most cases, I have found the fear of moving forward is exaggerated in our mind's eye until we actually start taking action toward our new direction.

Assess

One of the single most powerful tools we can use to inspire persistence is progress. Correlating actions with results gives you fuel to press on. My human behavior professor from Carnegie Mellon would remind us constantly, "If you can measure it, you can reward it; and if you can reward it, you will get it." That is the essence of this phase of changing a belief: learning to measure progress.

Some beliefs can be changed quickly (especially if you have someone like Instructor Aloha to guide you). Changing other beliefs can take a long time. And when that happens, I want you to learn to find progress in the actions you take. Progress can come from writing down each time you take a new action (such as a book log I created to document how many days a month I wrote). Or perhaps using a memory aid like a wristband you switch from one wrist to the next each time you take an empowering action toward accepting a new belief (I did that for incorporating more water into a new meal plan I adopted). Or maybe it is asking a friend to meet with you once a week to assess your improvement.

Changing a belief is as intentional as going after a goal. Many times I have found that the first actions I take toward a new goal start with the action of changing a limiting belief. Whether you're going after a new goal or changing a belief, you are using the same tools of self-awareness, progress assessment, and daily action to intentionally make something happen. These actions are the building blocks of self-leadership. The more you learn to lead yourself through change (that is the point of leadership: dealing with change), the more prepared and effective you will be at leading others.

Be creative about how you assess your progress. The sky is the limit on tracking your improvements; just know that you must define what it is you want to track. If you need a new belief of "I can still be the life of the party without alcohol," then come up with opportunities where you go to parties and have fun while drinking nonalcoholic drinks. If you need a new belief to help you climb your highest mountain ever, then find a series of mountains that you can climb while practicing how to prove to yourself you have what it takes. Accountability partners are great ways to help you stay on track with an honest assessment of your progress. Remember: Progress is progress. Regardless of how little progress you think you're making, it's still progress, and that is worth getting fired up about to keep trying!

Neutralize

By now you realize how important thoughts are to your future success. The thoughts we are attached to determine our directions over time. One of the best ways to flip a limiting belief into an empowering one is to embrace the new belief in the present tense through affirmations. For instance, if your goal is to be one of the top one hundred public speakers in the world, then make a belief affirmation that you repeat to yourself daily: "I am one of the top one hundred speakers in the world." The more you focus on this affirmation, the more you find yourself asking, "What can I do right now to make this affirmation my reality?" Changing beliefs is like achieving goals—success occurs from lots of tiny improvements.

James Clear, author of *Atomic Habits*, says, "All big things come from small beginnings. The seed of every habit is a single, tiny decision. But as that decision is repeated, a habit sprouts and grows stronger." He is right; the name of the belief-changing game is about making incremental changes that compound over time. One of the simplest and best changes you can make daily is developing and repeating a new belief affirmation. The process of building your new belief affirmation neutralizes the potency of the old one.

Remember that you can only focus on one thing at a time. If your focus is on your new belief affirmation, then it's stealing energy from the old, limiting one. Perfect! That is exactly what we want to happen. It's like dripping weed killer on a plant you do not want in your garden of beliefs. The more you fertilize the belief you want, the more you take energy from the belief you do not want. I call this final step in the I-CAN process *neutralize*, because that is exactly what you want to have happen: neutralize the old belief so it can no longer negatively impact your future success.

Here are few belief affirmations I have used to neutralize limiting beliefs and empower me to move forward toward my goals:

"I am a champion oarsman. I am built to row, and every stroke I take helps me get better."

"I am a great storyteller, and the stories I tell help people."

"I write books that are engaging to read and inspire people to succeed."

"I am great at walking up mountains. I am like a tractor that doesn't stop."

"I am the best speaker in the world."

"I am creative."

"I love my family, and I am always looking for ways to be a better dad, husband, son, and son-in-law."

Obviously, these are personal to me. There is only one person who matters when it comes to neutralizing your outdated beliefs: *you*! You must embrace your own belief affirmations. If you are having difficulty creating your own, then start by asking yourself, "What is it that I want to accomplish in the future?" For example, "I want to be a top one hundred recognized keynote speaker in the world."

After you've defined what it is you want, remove the future tense and replace it with the present tense: "I *am* a top one hundred recognized keynote speaker in the world." Write it down on a three-by-five card and carry it with you so you look at it several times a day. Remind yourself relentlessly of who you are. Create a routine of reminding yourself, such as repeating it to yourself every time you walk through a doorway or when you look in a mirror. The more you come to accept this new belief, the more you will take the necessary actions to make it your new reality.

Beliefs are within our control. Learning to cull and accept those beliefs that will help us achieve what we desire is one of the most important skills to learn. In the words of Instructor Half Butt, "It ain't complicated. It's just hard." I am here to reassure you that you *can* do it. You created the beliefs you have today, and you can create new ones that will help you achieve your next goals. As Henry Ford once said, "Whether you think you can or can't, you're right." Building an Unstoppable Mindset involves reminding yourself (and believing): **I CAN** do it!

EXERCISE | **Cutting the Anchor Chain**

I think of a limiting belief like a ship dragging an anchor. As much as you are trying to leave the harbor, you cannot because the anchor you are dragging is holding you back. Limiting beliefs are just like that—anchoring you to an old belief, perhaps something from your past that is preventing you from enjoying something in the present or future. The challenge with a belief is we believe it's true.

Here's the question: *What if* the belief is not true, *then what* would I do?

For instance, what if my asthma didn't limit me—what would I do? What if I am good at writing—what would I write? What if I am good at inventing things—what would I invent? What if I am good at public speaking—what would I speak about? All of these what-ifs were ones that I have personally learned to neutralize. But it is not easy at first because I believed them to be true. The first exercise is asking yourself the "what if/then what?"

This is a highly personal exercise that in the beginning you might not share with anyone, but over time I encourage you to share your answers with your closest swim buddy. The answers involve activating your imagination, envisioning what you would do if you *knew* you could do something that you believe you cannot. If the answer raises your heart rate and leaves you daydreaming about it over and over again, then guess what you are instinctively doing? You are making the fear of staying put greater than the fear of moving forward, which is exactly what you want to have happen when deciding to challenge your limiting belief. In essence, every time you envision the answer of "What if/then what?" you are taking a hacksaw to the old rusty anchor chain connected to that dragging anchor. The more you envision your future without that limiting belief, the faster you will cut through the anchor chain and set yourself free on an exciting new journey across the horizon to achieve a new dream!

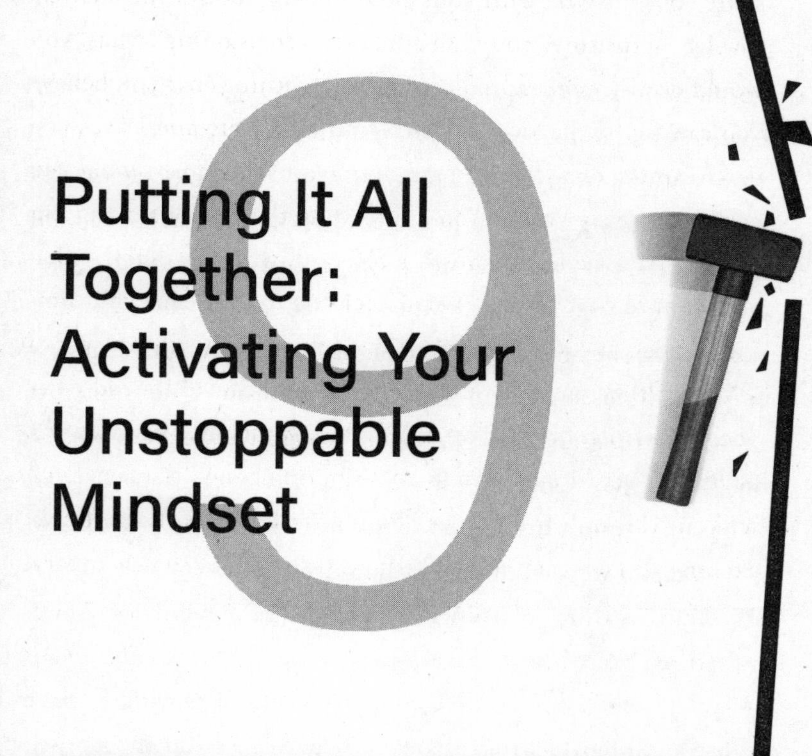

9 Putting It All Together: Activating Your Unstoppable Mindset

In the fall of 1991, with little more than two weeks of liberty left before I had to report to SEAL training in Coronado, my dad and I drove my VW from Massachusetts to San Diego. He had served in the Air Force during Vietnam in a special photo reconnaissance unit. He loved it. He was out of harm's way, but thrived on the detailed analysis required to find clues in the aerial photos of where POW camps and missile sites might be. I thought our trip across country would be spent discussing his military days, but instead he wanted to talk about anything and everything but his military experience. On the final day of our road trip, I was driving him to the San Diego airport so he could return to the East Coast when he finally broke his silence.

"Alden, I've been thinking about this day for months. I've racked my brain to think of things that might be helpful for you as you embark on your Navy SEAL journey. The fact is, I can't relate with it—the closest I can come to understanding it is what I saw in the before-and-after pictures of areas where SEALs did their missions. I have no tactical advice for you."

He trailed off for a moment and turned away from me. He was getting choked up, something I had never witnessed before. He turned back to me and said, "I have one thing I can offer: when you get stuck, give . . . Give all you have."

As I pulled up to the curb, I didn't quite know what to say, so I just nodded.

He turned to me and repeated with tears in his eyes, "You got it? When stuck, give—just go give, okay?" He hugged me and left.

In true Alden fashion, I did not get what he was talking about until months later when it looked like I was about to be medically dropped from SEAL training. Halfway through second phase, I was pulled out of a three-mile ocean swim because my lungs were bleeding. In the hospital, they discovered an antigen in my blood. The instructors raided my room and found my asthma medication. I had been sneaking it early in the morning and at night—using it as a crutch to help me through training.

While the training gods were deciding my fate, a newly minted SEAL officer friend of mine asked me if I wanted to help him with some volunteer work with the local Easter Seals foundation teaching paraplegics to swim. I had nothing else to do, so I went with him. If you know anything about paraplegics and swimming, the two don't really work well together. You don't teach them how to swim so much as you swim them. I loved it, and they clearly loved it too. I went back several times to swim with them.

During that time, I was also put through a battery of other pulmonary tests. It became clear that, should I be allowed to stay in training, I wouldn't be allowed to take any more asthma medications, since asthmatics are not allowed in the Navy. I was adamant that I wasn't an asthmatic, and to prove it, I threw out the medicines. Internally, I wasn't so sure about this decision. I had a long-term belief that I needed these medicines to perform. I was now faced with a decision of staying put—using the medicines would end my SEAL dream, but moving forward presented me with a major fear about whether I could perform without the medicine.

I never really prayed that much in my life until that moment. I began a nightly routine of praying that my lungs were strong enough without the medicine. I would pray for strength, for clear lungs, for open airways, for anything that would help me overcome my anchor belief that my lungs needed the medicine to stay healthy. I had run out of options, and found strength in practicing faith. Up until that moment, I had faith in my capabilities, but when I was no longer sure of my capabilities, I found comfort and strength in practicing faith in someone/something other than me—in my case, a higher power that I call God. The point is not to challenge where you put your faith, but instead to help you recognize the importance of faith and serving others.

I have come not to believe in coincidences anymore. Things happen for a reason. I passed the pulmonary tests and was eventually allowed to return to training, albeit I had to repeat many weeks of training (and spend time with Instructor Popeye). At the time, I never linked giving with my medical miracle of passing those lung tests. As the years have gone by and I have found myself stuck so many times I have lost count, I have found a major correlation between giving, serving, volunteering, and success. There are greater forces at work than you and I or even the scientific community have yet to define. However, several spiritual seekers over the millennia from Buddhists to Tibetan monks have known about this correlation between giving and succeeding, or in my case, getting unstuck. Their formula is called karma. Western philosophy calls it quantum mechanics. No matter which one you wish to believe, understand that both have come to realize that when you put forth an action, an equal and opposite reaction occurs. In the great loop of life, this holds true: the more you give, the more you receive.

In my experience, not all giving is equal. Giving for the sake of expecting a return will not get you what you want. Giving without expectation of return while giving of your greatest gift can have a force-multiplying effect. The magic of giving comes from giving the best of yourself—your gift.

We all have a gift, something unique and special to us. You will learn this gift as you cross your "ocean" toward your new goals. The gift will present itself as you struggle to overcome obstacles toward your goal. You will come to realize through your various struggles that there are some things that come to you effortlessly. In fact, you will start to look forward to those struggles because you like using your gift. Your unique talent requires work to refine it. You must practice it—it's not a perfectly polished, ready-to-go talent. It is raw, rough, and undeveloped, and requires that you face obstacles in order to refine it. This is another reason obstacles are so important to you—they will unlock your gifts, further activating your potential.

You might be asking yourself right about now, "Great, Alden, but I have no idea what my gift is. How do I find it?"

Here is a question for you to ask your closest swim buddies: "If I were going to save your life and I could only save your life using the one thing I'm best at, how would I save you?" Ask those same friends you used to triangulate your limiting belief, and focus on the verbs they provide you. For example, in my case, the gift I uncovered is to inspire. For my business partner Andrew Morrison, his gift is to analyze. Each of us has a gift, and the best ways to discover it are through the struggle of overcoming challenges and by giving back. These two are linked—the struggle in the face of the obstacles and the struggle to serve others. The obstacle refines your gift, and your service to others helps you practice your gift. Watch what happens over time when you use your gift not only to overcome obstacles but also to give back to others. Things will start to unexpectedly happen in miraculous and wonderfully mysterious ways. The German philosopher Johann Wolfgang von Goethe said:

Be bold and mighty forces will come to your aid.

I have experienced this time and time again. The act of being bold requires using your gift. The confidence you receive from knowing something you are uniquely good at helps drive you to take bold action. When you take bold actions, you will find bold responses, or, as Goethe puts it, "mighty forces" will come to support you. The challenge is taking that first bold action, which brings me full circle back to having faith in your dream.

Developing an Unstoppable Mindset starts with dreaming up a bold goal. After all, there is no reason to have an Unstoppable Mindset if you aren't seeking to do something you have never done before. Boldness is just that: going after something new to you, challenging yourself to go beyond what you originally thought was possible. Being bold means taking risks where there is real potential for failure. We are built to be bold, but taking bold action is our choice. The hard part is taking the bold action. You will often hear people talking about being bold, but actually taking the all-in action in a bold direction is quite a different story, and choosing to do so is the point of this chapter and for that matter the entire book!

This chapter puts it all together so you can understand how to make the mindset decisions to help you *be* bold and *stay* bold as you pursue your bold goal. Remember: You are the captain of your own ship, and you get to navigate your life. Let me share the Mindset Map to help you navigate through any obstacle. The Mindset Map is nothing more than how thoughts, focus, and beliefs influence each other to produce an action. As you read on, prepare yourself for the final exercise, for it's time to reevaluate the goals you named at the beginning of the book and then boldly set sail in the direction of your dreams!

THE MINDSET MAP

In much the same way you would not cross an ocean without a chart (map), you need a map to activate the potential of your mind. Throughout the chapters, I have shared each of the three components—thoughts, focus, and beliefs—that, when used in unison, can enable you to achieve more than you originally thought possible. Nothing happens overnight, and it takes time to practice making the little decisions that build into Unstoppable actions. Making incremental improvements is the name of the Unstoppable Mindset game, and here's the map to making the changes to Be Unstoppable in your goal-achievement journey.

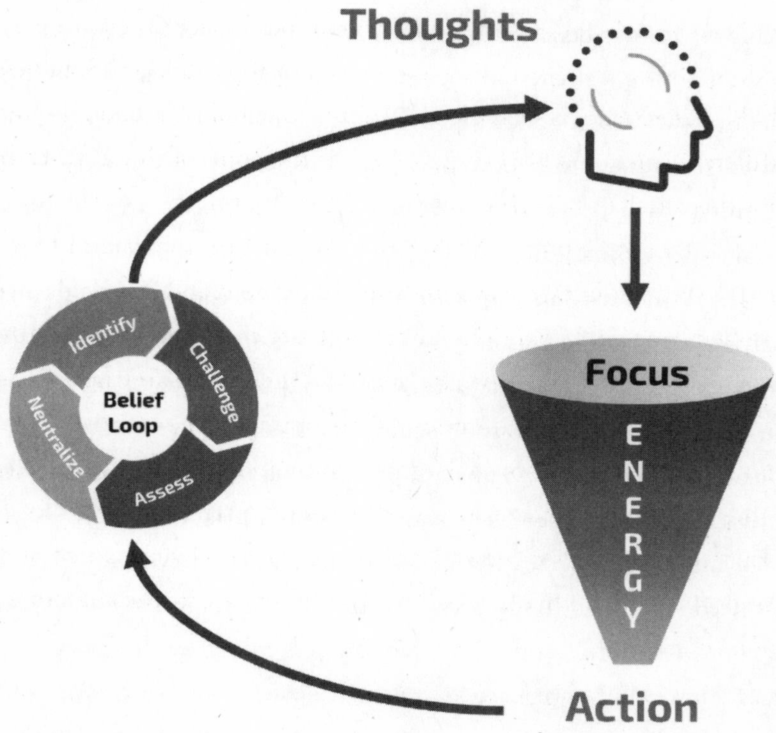

This book follows this map starting with thoughts and moving clockwise. I like starting with thoughts because choosing our thoughts is typically the first decision we make in a series of decisions to take an action. Remember: We generate untold numbers of thoughts every day. No thought is helpful or hurtful until we make the decision to attach our energy to it. We attach our energy via our focus, which I depict as a funnel. The stronger our focus, the more powerful our energy is toward that thought and the subsequent action we take. Moments after we take an action, we have another decision to make through an evaluation of deciding whether it was the correct action. While we are making that decision, we are seeking validation from our belief system. This is an important step because it is here we test our reasoning to believe (or not) in the actions we are taking. If we decide we do not believe our actions are worth the effort (and know we are fighting a perpetual force for putting forth the least amount of effort), we will abandon our efforts (i.e., give up). If, however, we recognize a reason to believe in our actions (e.g., I have rower's legs, therefore I will be good at rowing), then the process repeats with stronger determination.

The Mindset Map can work for or against the pursuit of your goal. Think of it like a spiral upward or downward depending on the thoughts you decide to attach to, where you put your focus, and what you decide to accept for your beliefs. It's a series of cascading decisions that can propel you upward or push you into a spiral of defeat. Activating our Mindset Maps happens through trial and error. I have failed many more times than I have succeeded. I have needed and still need swim buddies to pick me up when I question my ability to press on; I stumble, stall, and second-guess myself with the best of them. However, I have learned to use my goal-pursuing adventures to practice perhaps the most important ingredient of persistence: faith.

THE PURPOSE OF FAITH

The Oxford Dictionary offers up two definitions of faith. The first one refers to the ability to have 100 percent confidence in someone or something other than yourself. The second one is about faith as it pertains to religious doctrine. The definition I want to discuss is the first one. Practicing faith is much easier said than done. I believe in a higher power, and that higher power I believe in I call God. I am not here to convince you to accept my form of higher power. However, I do want you to appreciate that, in pursuit of achieving something you have never done before, there will be times when your only belief will come from someone or something other than yourself.

I have practiced faith many times over my lifetime from the battlefield to the boardroom to my children's bedroom. There have been times when all has seemed totally lost except my faith that some way, somehow I or we would find a way to succeed. Many times the solutions came about in roundabout ways that involved many more days, weeks, and even months of struggle. But keeping faith through the practice of believing in others and, yes, in a higher power, gave me just enough energy to press on. Similar to when I practiced faith while giving up my asthma medication, I found strength and courage in practicing faith in these situations.

If you have not figured it out by now, goal achievement is directly related to the actions you take. You can have the greatest plan on the planet, but nothing takes the place of persistent action toward your goal. It can be wildly frustrating when the actions you take seem to send you backward. When progress seems nonexistent and your goal appears unachievable, this is when faith can propel you forward. I appreciate that just using the word *faith* these days can act as a lightning rod for discourse on whose religious practice is more acceptable.

In my humble opinion, the basis for all religion is the ability for us to practice the fine art of faith in which we let go of limiting beliefs in pursuit of something greater than ourselves. When you learn to let go, you learn to empower others by putting your faith in them and committing your full agency to the action at hand.

CLOSING THE LOOP AND THE ESSENTIAL HUMAN TRINITY

As you practice faith, you will come to realize that faith is fueled by hope and love. Together, faith, hope, and love represent the essential power source of every single person. Whether you are leading yourself or a team over the horizon to a new goal destination, we need all three of these elemental ingredients to unleash our potential.

When discussing the Mindset Map and closing the loop between recognizing a reason to believe and taking another action, there can be a great divide between what you believe and the current thoughts you are attached to (e.g., "Can I take another action?" or "Is another action going to make a difference?" or "Is this worth it?"). This is especially important in the beginning of your pursuit of a new dream when you have not taken enough actions to show any substantive progress.

This beginning state is fragile and ripe for the many faces of fear to convince you to quit. To cross that divide you will need to build a bridge upon faith, hope, and love. I call these our human trinity, and with them we can walk through the deepest and darkest valleys of fear. You will be scared, perhaps even at times shaking and questioning your very resolve, but this trinity will give you a never-ending source of fuel to beat back fear while persevering toward your goal.

Think about it for a moment. Where does your love for your goal come from? Go back to chapter four, where I discussed the importance of purpose and passion. Those two are your ingredients for the love of the goal you seek. The more you practice linking your passion and purpose for your goal, the more you will discover your love for what it is you wish to achieve.

How about hope? Where does it come from? Hint: Remember when I discussed progress? Hope is based on progress or the future potential for progress. Link these two together, and the last remaining component is your ability to keep taking action even when you don't see the results you hope for. The fuel source for your ability to keep taking action? You guessed it: faith. When you link these together, you close the loop of the Mindset Map and give yourself a renewable source of unstoppable energy toward your goal.

OBSTACLES, STRUGGLES, AND STRENGTH

The fear of failure is quite often the first thing we think of when confronting a new obstacle. That is a normal reaction; after all, we are hardwired to survive. We place a much higher priority on surviving than we do on thriving. The chapters in this book are all focused on helping you do one thing: taking fully committed action in the face of seemingly insurmountable obstacles. I have offered tools, techniques, and frameworks to help you develop the courage and mindset to face down fear and take the next action. My hope for you is that over time you develop new habits that override your natural reflex of shying away from big, scary obstacles that prevent you from achieving your dreams.

I want you to appreciate what an obstacle is: an opportunity to grow. Obstacles provide us with the struggles we need to build the strength required to achieve our goal. Like working out in a gym with weights, our muscles need resistance to gain strength. In much the same way, we need resistance to test our resolve, to build our stamina, to improve our knowledge in order to achieve the goal we seek. Obstacles offer us the gifts of resistance we need to improve ourselves and accomplish what we want. Embrace the obstacle as the opportunity it represents—a chance to build strength and, while doing so, discover our true gift we can share with others. I consider this mindset shift one of the single most important Unstoppable Habits we can develop: embracing obstacles as opportunities to grow. When you view obstacles as growth opportunities, then you are well on your way to developing your own Unstoppable Mindset. The next step is taking daily action!

THE NUMBER ONE OBSTACLE

As I have mentioned many times before, we are imperfect. We cannot do it all. If you find yourself able to do it all, then I would challenge you to push yourself harder and leave your harbor of familiarity. If you can do it all, then you are not growing, and you aren't activating your full potential. As we seek to push ourselves out of the comfort zone of mediocrity, we will no doubt come face-to-face with our own perceived limitations.

Each one of us is born with inherent limitations. These limitations can present themselves in all kinds of ways. Maybe we have come to believe we are not good with numbers or can't draw or write a complete sentence. We all have limitations that we have either decided to accept or been told to accept by someone else. I want you to apply your Unstoppable Mindset to embracing this limitation as an opportunity to grow.

Without my diagnosis of asthma and my small lungs, I would not have pushed myself harder to overcome them. The discipline, hard work, and my learned ability to endure set in motion a series of cascading events that drive me to this day. I view my diagnosis as a gift. Though we all are imperfect and have all kinds of limitations, we also have innate gifts that, when activated, will propel us to use our full potential in accomplishing what we want. My ask of you is twofold: (1) challenge your limitations by embracing them as opportunities to help you develop new strengths, which will set you on your own path to Be Unstoppable toward your goals; and (2) as you discover your gift, do not reserve it for your personal enrichment, but give it without expectation of return to those in need on a weekly (or even daily) basis.

When you build a daily routine of serving others with your gift, you will begin to experience unusual coincidences. At first, you may say to yourself, *I got lucky*, but should you remain on a path of serving others with your gift, you will discover that "luck" will visit you often. Embrace it and be grateful for it but never stop giving your gift to others, for that is fuel that will power them and you to Unstoppable new experiences together, and there is no greater joy than when this happens.

The Final Exercise

As I mentioned in the beginning of this book, there will be a point when it is time to reevaluate your goals. This is that time. My goal is that as you have read and practiced the tools and techniques that I have shared with you, you have gained confidence in your natural born abilities. You are more powerful than you realize. You can do more than you originally thought possible. All you have to do is take one action at a time toward your goal. It only gets complicated when we start to think too much about what we can or cannot do.

This entire book is focused on one thing: inspiring you to take the next action. Each tool, technique, framework, and story is tailored to help you land your wheel of decision squarely on the one segment that reminds you minute by minute: I CAN!

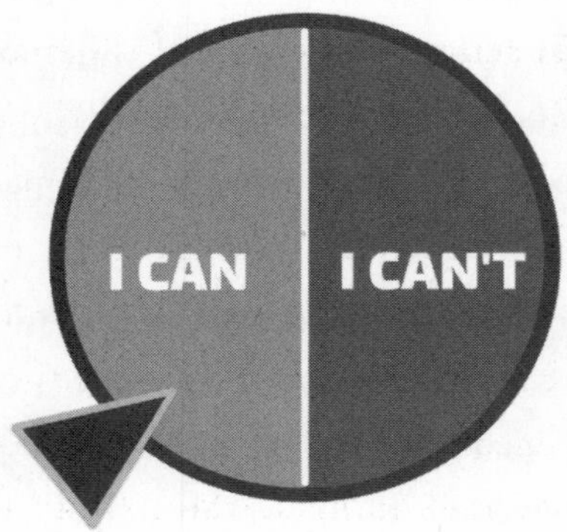

You are now armed with all kinds of weapons to fend off those many faces of fear attempting to convince you that you can't do something. You can and you will.

To help you on your goal journey, my swim buddy and I have developed a simple yet effective app called GoalBud. It's a free app that helps you take three major actions toward goal achievement:

1. Make a goal
2. Build a goal team
3. Create and report goal commitments

One of the biggest mistakes we make is attempting to go after a goal alone. Once you know the goal you want and why you want it, then take the next step by building your goal team.

It can be one person like we do in SEAL Team—our smallest team, the swim-buddy team—or it can be a thousand people supporting you on your goal journey. Use the GoalBud app to invite your buds and build your goal team. Once you have your team, create commitments of daily/weekly actions you will take and report your actions to your buds. Whether you're writing a book or climbing a mountain, the same rules apply—each goal is accomplished one word or one step at a time. No matter what it is you seek, it *always* come down to taking one action a time.

Review your ten-, three-, and one-year goals that you named at the beginning of the book. Are they the same or do you feel more encouraged to dream bigger? Regardless of your goal, now is the time to make the commitment to take new action toward that goal. Each time you take that action, know that you are incrementally improving yourself, your life, and the lives of those around you. Remember: Being unstoppable is a choice. You made a choice to read this book, and you can make the choice to Be Unstoppable at achieving your goal. I promise you that you are enough. You have what it takes, and the world needs you at your best! There is no time like the present: *Go Be Unstoppable* at living your dreams! See you over the horizon!

> Twenty years from now you will be more disappointed by the things you didn't do than by ones you did. So throw off the bowlines, sail away from the harbor. Catch the trade winds in your sails. Explore.
>
> —Mark Twain

ACKNOWLEDGMENTS

Going after a dream is hard work, but the hardest part is facing your fears during your journey to achieve your dream. The fear of doubt, wondering if you have what it takes, or questioning if you are enough, or if the dream is even achievable. The fear of failure and the embarrassment that comes with it. There is the fear of wasting your resources such as time, opportunity cost, and money. And then there is the constant fear of your ability to believe you can achieve it.

I battle these fears each and every time I set a course across the horizon to a new destination. I have learned over the years that you do not have to fight these many soldiers of fear alone. In fact, the most powerful foes to these combatants are people who believe in you and your dream. They love you for who you are, accept your limitations, remind you of your focus, and stand at the ready to answer your call when you stumble or fall.

Living your dreams is a team sport. Yes, your first team is the one inside your head—your mindset. But your external teammates are invaluable. They embrace your mindset and help you with the necessary course corrections to handle the inevitable obstacles along the way. These teammates I call my swim buddies.

There is no greater swim buddy than my wife, Jennifer Ryan Mills. Without her, this book would have never happened for it would be a one-dimensional story about my days as a SEAL platoon commander. We married while I was in SEAL Team, and for every success from that moment on, she has been my steadfast swim buddy. I could fill a book—perhaps I will—with her stories of support, guidance, and love, not to mention her leadership of raising four magnificent (and high-energy) boys.

Speaking of my boys, our four captains in training—Henry, Charlie, John, and William—you are the reason I write. There is no greater gift you give me (and Mom) than listening to us and, at times, taking our advice. In the darkest valleys of writing doubt, you and your willingness to journey after your own dreams are what inspire me to keep writing. Mom and I are in awe of you and your courage to pursue your dreams.

The foundation of this book began in 1884 when my great-grandfather was born. At twelve years of age, he broke his arm so badly that he could no longer work on the family farm. His parents and a benefactor helped him get an education. He eventually founded a company while serving in support roles in two world wars. My parents ensured I spent time with him nearly every week until he died (ninety-eight years old). I knew him for fourteen years. My mom and dad are storytellers. They always find ways to weave something from my family heritage into helping me believe my dream is achievable. Mom and Dad, you set my mindset in motion.

Along with my biological parents, I am blessed to have another set of parents, Joe and Kathy Ryan (aka Pops and Mumzie), who are unconditional in their support, encouragement, guidance, and love. The Perfect Pushup (and the products that followed), the books, the overseas dreams, and so much more would not have happened without their swim-buddy support.

Unstoppable Mindset was a book I wanted to write for over five years. Jud Laghi (aka J-Train) patiently took every one of my calls, listened to my numerous ideas, and helped craft this book's course to reality. He also helped me find a new swim buddy publisher named Matt Holt. With Matt's support and unwavering belief, along with a team of swim-buddy editors in Katie Dickman, Paul Felton, and Richard Rawson, they helped guide me across a new book horizon. Thank you to my editing swim buddies. I am so grateful for your guidance.

As I mentioned in the introduction, this book would not have been possible without a series of coaches, mentors, partners, guides, and in some cases just pure angels who would arrive serendipitously at just the right time in my life. In no particular order, these people represent special swim-buddy support; they are: Professor Gilmore, William H. Armstrong, W. Hart Perry Jr., Eric Houston, Rick Clothier, Rodney Pratt, Navy Crew Brotherhood, SEAL Instructors of Classes 181 and 182, Doug Lowe and Dave Morrison, Bart O'Brien, The Guardsmen, Brett Bush, Chip Pyfer, Andrew Morrison, Colin Murray, Ilya Yacobson, Josh White, John Bush, Forum X, Barbara Caraballo, Jack Bickel, and J. D. Messinger.

There is one more fear I battle every time I write a book: leaving out an acknowledgment. I am certain I have missed someone, for there have been so many over my lifetime who have made me who I am to date. For those I have missed, I am sorry, but not to worry—you are not forgotten forever, just for the deadline of this book!

For all my swim buddies, *thank you* for your unstoppable support. You inspire me and remind me daily that being Unstoppable is a choice. And finally, my hope to every reader out there—may this book inspire you to set sail courageously over the horizon to new and exciting destinations.

I believe in you.

Alden

ABOUT THE AUTHOR

Kathleen Harrison Photo

Alden Mills is an author, speaker, and coach focused on helping people be unstoppable at achieving their goals. His work has appeared in *Forbes*, *Entrepreneur*, *Fast Company*, and on *CBS This Morning*. He regularly speaks to and coaches Fortune 500 companies as well as other companies and organizations seeking to make a difference in the world.

His diverse leadership background as a nationally ranked D1 athlete, three-time Navy SEAL platoon commander, *Inc. 500* CEO/founder, and inventor (with more than forty worldwide patents), along with his uncanny ability to inspire and coach, makes him a highly sought-after speaker and executive coach.

With more than thirty years of leadership experience, Alden has cultivated a methodology—Unstoppable Leadership—that develops people into congruent and authentic leaders who successfully build teams and create cultures that are unstoppable regardless of the situation, industry, or environment.

He believes everyone is a leader and is more powerful than they realize. His passion is helping people activate their potential to do more than they originally thought possible. When he is not helping others succeed, he spends every available moment with his wife, four boys, and two Labs in Northern California.

Congratulations!

You're well on your way to being unstoppable in pursuing your dreams. But the journey to success doesn't end here. It's an ongoing process that requires unwavering effort and dedication. That's why we're here—to provide constant support every step of the way.

From practical advice to valuable tools, our mission is to keep you motivated and focused on your goals, no matter the challenges. Join our community at ***UnstoppableMindsetBook.com*** or scan the QR code below to reach new heights of success!

Charlie Mike.